WHY
GOOD PEOPLE
DO
BAD THINGS

WHY
GOOD PEOPLE
DO
BAD THINGS

ERWIN W. LUTZER

WORD PUBLISHING

NASHVILLE

A Thomas Nelson Company

Published by Word Publishing, a Thomas Nelson, Inc., company,
P. O. Box 141000, Nashville, Tennessee 37214.

ISBN 0-8499-1667-4

Printed in the United States of America
01 02 03 04 05 06 PHX 9 8 7 6 5 4 3 2 1

CONTENTS

INTRODUCTION

WHEN EVA BRAUN'S HOME MOVIES of Adolf Hitler were discovered, some objected to them being released to the public. The critics argued that the movies humanized Hitler; they made him appear so "normal" within the context of everyday life. The objectors did not want people to see him smiling, playing with his dog, or tousling the hair of a four-year-old girl. They preferred that he be remembered as one mysteriously aloof from the common delights of other mortals; they wanted to retain the fiction of a nonhuman Hitler.

But the fact is, Hitler was human—perhaps too human. The seeds of his hatred and egomania did not reside in him alone but can be found in the lives of many who dominate the pages of history. Yes, the number of people who have committed crimes on a massive scale is relatively small. But history has proved that there are thousands of Hitlers, some more famous than others, others equally wicked but lacking the resources to carry out their diabolical plans. No, Hitler is not an aberration, for the blood of humanity ran through his veins. If you think that his ilk no longer exists on the face of the earth, just read today's newspaper!

Though we cringe at Hitler's crimes, many people have never seriously grappled with the fact that any one of us, given the right combination of desires and circumstances, is capable of evil—even great evil, the kind that we are quick to condemn in others. We are both naive and dishonest if we do not take into account the obvious fact that even in so-called good people, the potential for evil on a grand scale lies dormant.

A MYSTERY

"I think every person is a mystery, and it's strange to me that a person I grew up with and was very close with remains one of the greatest mysteries of all." These are the words of the mild-mannered David Kaczynski when speaking of his brother, Ted, the so-called Unabomber, who was responsible for planting bombs on university campuses, killing several people.[1] Yes, every person is a mystery, and it is this mystery we seek to probe in the following pages.

The mystery, of course, can be simply stated: Why is it that we as members of the human race, who have such great capacities for achievement in art, science, and compassionate sacrifice, have within us the seeds of greed, hatred, egomania, and destruction? Pascal speaks of our struggle: "True religion must teach that there is in man some fundamental principle of his greatness, as well as some greatly rooted principle of his misery."[2] Greatness and misery—that is our story, the story of the human race.

The matter is complicated because the line between greatness and misery—between the good and the bad—is often blurred due to the fact that the same person is capable of both. For example, by any standard Picasso was a genius of staggering proportions. Yet, his private life was in shambles, and worse, he abused those around him with arrogant disdain. His first wife, Olga, went insane; his mistress Marie-Therese Walter hanged herself; a second mistress suffered a nervous breakdown; his second wife, Jacqueline, shot herself to death. Robert Rosenblum, who has made Picasso the object of detailed study, comments, "This man, with irresistible charm, manipulative self-promotion and shocking cruelty, changed the life of every person he met."[3]

Irresistible charm! Shocking cruelty! This dual aspect of man fosters his delusions. Though he can see the evil in others, he concentrates on the good when evaluating himself. Thus, as we shall see, some people are blind to their own faults and appear incapable of honest evaluation. They hide not only from God and others, but also from themselves.

I doubt that some children are born with a greater degree of original sin than others. That some have an obvious propensity to perversity as they grow older is clear enough, but we all know people—good people—who have done some very bad things. We all have been shocked by friends, churchgoers, and relatives from the finest of homes who have not lived up to our expectations. Shakespeare was right when he said, "Good wombs hath borne bad sons." Reflect for a moment:

- We've known ministers, with a reputation for being kind and loving, who have abandoned their wives and children for another lover.
- We've known otherwise reputable people who have pilfered funds from bank accounts, doctored checkbooks, or stolen money outright.
- We've known those who in the interest of self-protection have destroyed those around them with lies, distortions, and cunning schemes.
- We've known people who have become addicted to power, sex, drugs, or alcohol.
- We all have known—if we were totally honest—that we have had the potential of doing greater evil if we had not been restrained by the expectations of our friends, the laws of the land, and most important, the grace of God. As Solzhenitsyn said, the line between good and evil is not drawn through the human race, but through every human heart. There is a mixture of the good, the bad, and the ugly in us all. Seneca declared, "Man gazes at the stars but his feet are in mud." Because we are capable of falling into the mud, Scripture reminds us, "If you think you are standing firm, be careful that you don't fall!" (1 Cor. 10:12).

We have to fear our own hearts. It would take only a few minutes for any one of us to destroy our reputation, ruin our marriage, and cause our friends to lose their respect for us. No wonder Luther said that he feared his own heart more than he did the pope!

THE HUMAN HEART

The purpose of this book is to shine a light on the human heart, to honestly admit to our own deceptions and sins. The more aware we are of our need, the more appreciative we will be for God's gracious intervention to save us from ourselves. There is plenty of hope on these pages for the criminal, as well as for the self-respecting churchgoer who really can't think of anything he has done wrong in, say, the last five years. As we shall learn, the latter might need more help than the former!

Keep this in mind as you read.

First, this is not a textbook on psychology as such. The insights of psychology are helpful for analysis, but psychology cannot prescribe a cure for what ails us. My contention is that with few exceptions, psychology has not taken evil as seriously as it should. And even those who have plumbed the depths of human nature have not found the key to the transformation of the human heart. God, who entered our world through Christ, is the only One who can forgive us, change our desires, and fill our aching void. We must not believe the lie that we are incapable of change.

Second, I believe that only the Bible has the correct analysis of the human heart; indeed, the insights of the inspired text square with experience. When scientists exulted in the news that they had finished sequencing the human genome, it sounded as if we would have to rethink what it means to be human. An article in the *Chicago Tribune* asked, "Is there a gene for the human soul?"[4] But alas—though this first draft of the so-called human book of life might be of immense help in curing physical sickness—there is no DNA that can spell out the components of the soul. Love, hate, creativity, and the like are beyond the range of our genetic map. If we are to be changed, we will have to appeal to ourselves and to others, but most of all to God. And only the Bible points the way.

I think it was Chesterton who wondered why liberal theologians denied original sin, when it was the only doctrine that could be proved by reading a daily newspaper! Jesus said of us all, "What comes out of a man is what makes him 'unclean.' For from within, out of men's hearts, come evil thoughts, sexual immorality, theft, murder, adultery, greed, malice, deceit, lewdness, envy, slander, arrogance and folly. All these evils come from inside and make a man 'unclean.'" (Mark 7:20–23).

Third, although God can and does change the human heart, we must ruefully admit that even those who have experienced His transforming grace often do bad things. I wish there were a neat and visible distinction between those who have come to trust Christ as Savior and those who have not. Unfortunately, we've all met Christians who have lapsed into sinful patterns that seem to belie their faith in Christ. However, we should note this: God disciplines His children who live in willful disobedience. Indeed, if someone is without such discipline, he in point of fact proves that he is not a believer after all (see Heb. 12:7–8). No one—including devoted Christians—becomes perfect in this life, but those who have experienced what Jesus called "the new birth" are expected to demonstrate it by a change in lifestyle and behavior.

It is imperative that we face ourselves in the presence of God and become radically devoted to Him so that His transforming power can work in us and through us. Analysis must precede cure for the simple reason that we do not know what the remedy should be until we understand the disease. If we are people of few faults then a superficial cure might do, but if we are at root self-deceived then we need stronger medicine. I offer this book to you as an assessment of our condition, along with the prescription that God has provided through His grace and power.

As we know, there are medical plans that will not help those who have a preexisting condition. When it comes to sin, we all have a preexisting condition. We are born as sinners, and as we grow up, we act out our fallenness with varying degrees of intensity. But Christ came into the world to "save his people from their sins" (Matt. 1:21). We need not fear what is in our hearts if we believe that God's grace is greater than all our problems.

Join me on a journey. Just as a visit to the doctor might be unpleasant, so God's diagnosis of our hearts might be painful; but the pain precedes the cure. Yes, God wounds us that He might heal us, and He smites us down that we might be raised up. In His own words, "See now that I myself am He! There is no god besides me. I put to death and I bring to life, I have wounded and I will heal, and no one can deliver out of my hand" (Deut. 32:39). With a God like that, we can be assured of help for our need.

Invite Him to join you on this journey of self-discovery.

CHAPTER 1
LOST IN A HOUSE OF MIRRORS

Only god knows who i really am and may he graciously preserve me from finding out!" said Johann von Goethe, the scholar of the German Enlightenment. He knew that self-discovery can be very painful; what he might not have known is that such a search can lead to fulfillment and peace.

Self-perception lies at the heart of our attitudes and behaviors. Give a four-year-old boy a cowboy hat, and he will ride every piece of furniture in the house. Give a girl a doll, and she will perceive herself to be a mother and act accordingly. A Lutheran minister told his seminarians that they should always wear their clerical collar because they would be much less likely to purchase pornography or fall into immorality if they had a constant reminder of who they were.

Marilyn Monroe grew up in foster homes, believing that she was fundamentally unloved and unlovable. This deeply rooted self-perception drove her to reach out for love in the only way she knew. Becoming a "sex object" was the price she paid for winning the love and adoration she craved. But the cost was too high; her attempts to win love made her feel empty and used. She believed (quite rightly, as it turns out) that she was loved for her body, not because she had value as a person. She died a suicide, feeling abandoned and unloved. I'm reminded of the woman who told me, "My father told me I was trash, so I lived like trash and fulfilled his perception of me."

If it is true that self-perception affects our behavior, how can we find out who we really are? Where do we turn to embark on the path of self-discovery? And since, down deep within, we are often quite different from our public persona, how can we really know who we are?

A VISIT TO THE HOUSE OF MIRRORS

At a county fair I ventured into a "fun house," a house of mirrors, where each wall made me look different. In one room I looked tall and skinny, in another fat and short. I walked into a hallway and my head was enlarged; I took a few steps toward another mirror and my abdomen was huge, but my head was small. Some mirrors projected an image that made me only slightly distorted; others made me hopelessly lopsided. One room made me lose weight, and in another I gained a hundred pounds. I was glad that in the last room there was a mirror that reflected what I really looked like.

What if the whole world were a house of mirrors and we found ourselves going from one to another trying to guess which was the "truth" about us? Our temptation would be to choose the mirror that makes us look the best, whether or not it reflected reality.

We're all on a search for a mirror that will make us look good to ourselves, to others, and to God. We yearn to project an image according to our own liking. We want people to see what we want them to see, nothing more, nothing less. If reality is not according to our liking, we will find a mirror that suits us and hope that others will believe the distortion. We will choose friends who tell us exactly what we want to hear and shun those who do not make us "feel good about ourselves." We will seek all those things that give us significance and when necessary separate our private life from our public persona.

In an article titled "Public Saints, Private Sins," *World* magazine discussed what should be done when people who espouse family values don't live up to their principles. We've all been disappointed by Christian leaders who have been "saints abroad and devils at home."[1] All of us face the temptation of saying one thing and doing another. Though we might be greedy and selfish, we are tempted to go to great lengths to appear generous and kind. Even if we are filled with lust and deceit, we may project an image of moral uprightness and a commitment to integrity. The basest of actions can be cloaked with religious fervor or lofty devotion. What matters is appearances.

Facing the reality of who we are is difficult; in this book we will discover that some of us appear incapable of owning up to our true desires and motives. We'll describe people who flee from reality, terrified lest their true self be exposed. And yet, unless we are willing to face the truth about ourselves, we can never be helped since honesty turns out to be the path to forgiveness, meaning, and a personal security. But I'm ahead of the story.

How do we perceive who we are? We're all born into a house of mirrors. Early in life we see our reflection in the words and deeds of those who interact with us. And those early self-perceptions have a great deal to do with our ability and willingness to embark on the path of self-discovery.

How can we begin on that path?

MIRRORS WE HAVE KNOWN

Family

The parents (or other adult caregivers, in some cases) serve as the first mirror in which children see themselves. In a healthy home, in which love, order, and respect are present, children have a much improved chance of growing up with a sense of personal well-being and value as they identify with and see these qualities represented and practiced in their "mirrors." Being surrounded by supportive and interested family members (immediate and extended) enables a young child to withstand the onslaught of the outside world, even if he is demeaned by teasing or ridiculed for some physical or mental peculiarity. If a child has parents and family who think he is okay, he can manage insults from others, including peers. Yes, he hurts, but the pain is manageable, for he knows he has special value. I agree with Mark Epstein, who wrote, "Parents who can allow a child to hate them temporarily, who can survive that hatred and return love, are bestowing the greatest of gifts."[2] A child with such parents is blessed indeed.

Another benefit of a healthy home is that young people who are encouraged to mirror the values of commitment and communication often take those values into work and marriage. Of course, it is human nature to fall short of what we know, but if strong models of integrity and love are present, at least the knowledge of what a functional home should look like is obtained.

Now let's change the scenario. If a home is abusive or if the parents are addicted to alcohol or drugs, a child will grow up in an environment with a code of silence; there is the unwritten rule that one does not talk about the family problems. Conflicts are left unresolved and all the emotions put on "autopilot."

Regrettably, many parents are unable to equip their children to live as whole adults. When I speak of a "whole adult," I mean someone who is able to give and receive love, someone who is capable of relating to others in meaningful ways. Many adult children of divorce and abuse cannot show love, for in doing so they would have to reveal a part of themselves they would prefer to keep hidden.

Recently, I read of a father who angrily said to his son, "You are nothing but the product of a one-night fling!" The biting words were intended to destroy the child. The father knew that he could not kill his son without significant social and legal consequences to himself. So he did the one thing he could get away with: He killed the spirit of the child by belittling him and cutting at the heart of his self-worth. Such children grow up with what I call the "big three" emotional burdens: shame, anger, and self-condemnation.

The impact of parenting on a child is enormous. Children are not in a position to compare their parents with other parents; therefore, the parents are like gods to them. The children will assume that their parents are an accurate mirror of who they (the children) are. In his book *People of the Lie*, M. Scott Peck writes, "If treated badly by the parents, the child will assume that it is bad. Raised without love, children come to believe themselves unlovable. Whenever there is a major deficit in parental love, the child will, in all likelihood, respond to that deficit by assuming itself to be the cause of the deficit, therefore developing an unrealistically negative self-image."[3] Children of evil parents think that the evil resides in them, not in their parents. And, if they think of themselves as evil—perhaps even criminals—they will act out their perception.

Children often mask their anger and hurt to manage parental expectations, and this mask hardens into a shell. They must stay behind the mask to hide their feelings, knowing that their parents cannot handle the full impact of their anger and hurt. Their playacting is a form of dishonesty that becomes the price of acceptance. But as long as the shell is maintained, they never learn how to show love or receive it. When confronted with God's grace and love, they want to turn away. If their parents didn't love them, they reason, why would God? And, by the way, where was He when they were growing up as targets of such abuse and pain?

To them the notion of God's acceptance is that it's for nice people who get good grades and attend church. Or, they may believe that grace is only for the people who can afford a new car and have enough money to ski in Aspen. But for the person who feels self-loathing, nothing much matters. Such have already made up their minds that they are losers. The temptation to resort to drugs, alcohol, and sex to deaden the pain of emptiness is overwhelming.

On the flip side, these people are often most responsive to God's grace once they grasp it. Many of them discover, as David did, that good parenting is not absolutely essential for a life of meaning and hope. "Though my father and mother forsake me, the LORD will receive me" (Ps. 27:10). Grace is good news for those who have nothing to bring to God.

Important Others

The second mirror that reflects a child's identity is his interaction with others. A child who is treated badly at home may derive some hope, some reason to live, from the kindness of a teacher, neighbor, or friend. A supportive relationship with others might be the first glimmer of hope that perhaps he is worth the trouble of caring for and has some value.

Dorie Van Stone was sexually abused both as a child in an orphanage and as a teenager in a foster home. During those dark days, she had one small ray of hope: A proprietor in a drugstore would always greet her cheerily and let her have a malt without paying for it. A few moments in that corner drugstore were a welcome relief from the uncaring strife of a dysfunctional family. Her damaged self-perception was given a glimmer of hope through this small act of kindness, which was never forgotten.[4]

There are other mirrors that reflect back to us who we are: a marriage partner, friends, the church. In each case, for good or ill, we gain insights about ourselves that will impact our attitudes and behaviors. Intuitively, we want honest feedback, and yet it can also be scary. It is one thing to have an honest opinion; it is quite another to have honest feedback regarding the thoughts and motives of the heart!

Early on, we learn that we can enhance our image on the outside by hiding our true self from the world. As children, we discover that it is possible to be one thing on the outside and something else on the inside. I personally learned that at about the age of ten. Out on the farm it was my responsibility to feed the chickens at five o'clock every afternoon. One day at around five-thirty, I walked into the garage and my father asked me if I had fed the chickens. Feeling very embarrassed and not wanting to risk his displeasure, I said, "Yes, I did."

Ten minutes later, I left the garage and secretly did my duty. I can remember congratulating myself on how easy it was to lie and mentally giving myself reasons why I would do it again, when convenient. But my elation was short-lived: My brother had overheard my conversation with my father and just happened to see me later feeding the chickens. He confronted me and told me I'd better stop my deceit because "God was watching." As best I remember, that ended my lying career.

Many others aren't that fortunate. They've had the misfortune of getting by with their deceptions. A small lie leads to more lies, and eventually more lies lead to bigger lies. Within time a whole web of deceit is carefully crafted, controlled, and hidden. As Sir Walter Scott wrote, "O, what a tangled web we weave, when first we practice to deceive!"

The Swiss theologian Karl Barth has rightly pointed out that we are all incorrigible liars. Because we live under the dominion of sin, we lie to God, to ourselves, and to others. We will fight against any encroachment of light that uncovers the hidden closets of the soul. As that secret dark side of our lives flourishes, we will look around, trying to find one mirror after another that will give us significance. We will pursue wealth, power, and beauty in an attempt to hide our insecurities and the emptiness we feel on the inside.

Some may become like Dr. Jekyll and Mr. Hyde: One part of us is meticulous in giving the appearance of rightness; another part can be evil and cunning. It is not true that "what you see is what you get." Just ask the woman who marries a loving man only to discover after the wedding that he is angry and abusive. Every one of us is like the moon, with a dark side that no one sees. We all agree that if our secret thoughts, motives, and deeds were known, we would be terrified. We would all want to flee to a deserted island.

MAINTAINING THE FALSE SELF

It is impossible to exaggerate the amount of psychic energy that some people use to manage the discrepancy between who they are within and their public persona. Within, there may be deep feelings of shame, inadequacy, rejection, and anger, but the truth cannot be revealed. Perhaps the person is hiding an addiction, a deception, or a crime. At all costs this must be hidden, and a false self is created that must be meticulously maintained, regardless of who gets hurt, regardless of how many lies are either told or covered.

Denial

The first line of defense is denial, that is, the filtering of all information that comes to our psyche so that people see in us only what we want them to see. We try to hide who we are, either to mask pain or to avoid shame. The deeper the denial, the more consistently all our judgments reflect the false image we assume is the truth about us; everything else is denied. The mind is used to block all information that is unfavorable or puts us in a negative light.

Sometimes we hide a part of ourselves under a cloak of religious commitment and fervor. For example, Ananias and Sapphira pretended that they gave all the proceeds of the sale of their land to the early church when, in point of fact, they had only given a part of its price. Thus they lied, not only by denying their inner greed, but also by projecting an image of generosity. According to the account in the New Testament, God was not amused at their hypocrisy and, as a result, they died (see Acts 5:1–10).

Psychologists speak of conscious denial, that is, those who are deceptive and know it. We think for example of the man who habitually uses pornography but hides it to make sure that his dreaded secret is never exposed. An alcoholic might swear his family to secrecy, warning of the consequences if they were to expose the truth about his addiction. Criminals, for the most part, know that they are deceivers; thus, they meticulously hide their behavior. Yet they cannot bring themselves to admit they have done wrong; the real problem is that "no one understands" them.

But there is also unconscious denial. This happens when there is a genuine deception, that is, when the person believes his own lies because the truth has been pushed to his subconscious. A man might have lied so much about his sins and crimes that he actually believes he did not molest the child, he did not steal, or he is not an addict. Of course, denial is not limited to just criminals, but finds a home in all our hearts. At times my wife has graciously pointed out my faults, but often I "just don't get it" because, quite frankly, I don't want to get it. But the more honest I become the more I realize that she is right—painfully right.

By definition, we don't see our own "blind spots." I know a man who had a huge blind spot, denying his anger, selfishness, abusiveness, and the like. Everything he did was "right" according to his reasoning. He did not realize that when he lashed out at others, he was describing his own faults! Stone-blind to his own sins, he was capable only of magnifying the faults of others. His reality-check bounced!

Some people feel wonderful about themselves because they have chosen a mirror that reflects exactly what they want to see. Denying the ugly part of themselves and arming themselves with a carefully crafted shell of protection, they believe the false image they project. The Bible speaks of such a man: "For in his own eyes he flatters himself too much to detect or hate his sin" (Ps. 36:2). So self-absorbed, he cannot detect his sin! Aquinas describes some people as having "cultivated ignorance," that is, an ignorance that is carefully protected for frequent use.

Wealth and Power

While some people have a healthy sense of self-worth, others only try to create great net worth. The tycoon on Wall Street, with millions he could never spend, may be caught cheating to make more millions. His acquisition of wealth is where he finds his significance; this is his way of covering deep personal inadequacies and "being somebody." The thought of being stripped of his wealth and power is terrifying since his real self with all of its weaknesses would be exposed; thus, the game must go on.

Others cover their false self by the accumulation of things, whether they can afford them or not. Their desire to impress those around them, without revealing their own insecurities, leads them to project a life of luxury and excess, even if it plunges them into debt. Those reared in poverty, who often felt shamed and inadequate in early life, thus become workaholics, determined never to be belittled again. An obsession with money and the need for personal security cover deep insecurities. Some will not dare peek out from behind their false self to face the anger and hurt within.

We've all met those who draw their primary significance from other people. Thus they will take extraordinary steps to meet the rich and famous or aspire to friendships that will enhance their own sense of importance. In their minds, their friends can do no wrong; but should these friends disappoint them, they will be vilified as enemies. What they are saying is, "You are my friend only as long as you give me significance, but after that, you are my enemy; there is no neutral ground."

So desperate are some people for significance that they will greatly exaggerate their estimation of who they are, even in ways that stagger the imagination. I know a man who contributed little by way of his gifts and abilities to the benefit of his company, but in his eyes he was indispensable, the one to be thanked for its every success. Incredibly, he actually appeared to believe his self-aggrandizement. He perceived his contribution to be so critical that when he was fired for incompetence, he predicted the demise of the whole business. But as you might guess, with him gone, the company did even better.

Physical Attractiveness

Most impressions formed of us are based on our appearance. In James Dobson's words, beauty "is the gold coin of human worth." Beautiful people get more attention and are given the benefit of the doubt in any controversy. I read a story about a young man who was acquitted of rape, not for lack of evidence (it was overwhelming), but because he looked so good—so clean-cut—the jury could not believe that this "handsome, all-American boy" could have committed such a crime. Since our society worships the human body, those who are of average or below-average appearance feel rejected, overlooked, and second-class.

In a society obsessed with beauty, many women especially find themselves threatened by the bombardment of female images in all forms of the media. For many, attractiveness is the mask that covers deep insecurities and the false self that cannot be revealed. Some are obsessed with the constant need for attention, thus go from lover to lover trying to affirm their value.

Those women who are of ordinary appearance have this advantage: They probably never did depend upon their beauty for their self-esteem. Those who derive their self-worth from their attractiveness not only must doubt that they are loved for who they are, but also must face the reality that beauty does not last forever. It is reported that Maria Montez, a popular film star of the 1940s, was so intoxicated with her own beauty that she drowned herself in a bathtub because she could not bear the thought of old age.

Comparison to Others

Those who feel inadequate often resort to comparing themselves to those who are more gifted and qualified than they. Desperate to retain some sense of significance and feeling diminished by those who outshine them, they resort to ridicule, criticism, and slander. The slightest fault in a perceived rival is magnified, and whatever facts can be twisted, will be. They are thinking (perhaps subconsciously), *If I can destroy those who outshine me . . . if I can cut them down to size, I will stand a bit taller among the ruins.*

Most distressing are those who attack others with accusations that actually apply to themselves. A woman was routinely critical of all those who tried to help her, accusing them of being unloving, uncaring, and hypocritical. She spoke angrily to all who would listen, interpreting even the most helpful gestures of others toward her as inadequate and based on wrong motivations. All attempts to win her over with love failed. Those who knew her well could not help but notice that every complaint against others was a description of herself. Such people deny their own woundedness and do not realize that they project their own attitudes onto others. I'm reminded of the story of the drunk whose friends smeared a strong-smelling cheese under his nose while he was drinking in a bar. He staggered out into the clear night and complained, "The whole world stinks!"

Sometimes self-deception borders on mental illness. A volunteer on a committee to research the expansion of a Christian campus voted in approval with the recommendation his colleagues had made. But days after the vote, he turned against the committee, including the president of the school, making accusations of dishonesty, manipulation, and corruption. When asked for evidence, he said that he had no need of proof since the "Holy Spirit" had revealed these things to him! Turns out, these accusations were a picture of him, not the committee. What made it so insidious is that, at times, he could quote Scripture, pray with intensity, and otherwise give the impression of being a committed Christian. Equally distressing is the fact that he seemed to honestly believe his slanderous charges!

Religious Legalism

The false self often hides behind apparent righteousness. But those people who are focused on the letter of the law lack a heart of devotion to God and are always critical of those who appear to be overstepping the boundaries. The legalist has his own set of rules, such as the proper hair length, the proper attire for church, the dos and don'ts of entertainment, and the like. He is especially angry with those who break his rules and still appear to be blessed by God. His rules are front and center, and woe to those who don't see outward conformity as primary.

Jesus was constantly encountering people whose impeccable public self was a shield for greed, covetousness, lust, and above all, self-aggrandizement. Listen to His stinging rebuke:

> Everything they do is done for men to see. . . . They love the place of
> honor at banquets and the most important seats in the synagogues;
> they love to be greeted in the marketplaces and to have men call

them "Rabbi." . . . Woe to you, teachers of the law and Pharisees, you hypocrites! You clean the outside of the cup and dish, but inside they are full of greed and self-indulgence. . . . You are like whitewashed tombs, which look beautiful on the outside but on the inside are full of dead men's bones and everything unclean. (Matt. 23:5–7, 25, 27)

On the outside they appeared righteous, but inside, Jesus said, they were "full of greed and wickedness" (Luke 11:39).

Adam Smith wrote, "This self-deceit, this fatal weakness of mankind, is the source of half of the disorders of human life."[5] Underneath the external facade is an emptiness, a sense of fear, and a need to keep one's private self hidden, lest the hollowness within be exposed. If we deny our hurt, our anger, and our self-doubt, we can become emotionally numb and soon believe any lie that the heart insists we believe. We should fear lest we become content with our self-deceptions, for then we shall never be reconciled to God. Repentance is nothing more than admitting our deceit in the presence of God and receiving His mercy for the lies we have believed about ourselves.

My wife and children enjoy putting puzzles together. They begin with a thousand or more pieces scattered randomly across a table with no clues as to how the pieces can possibly fit together. Only one thing guides them: the picture on the box. As they focus on what the end product should look like, they have enough information to make intelligent decisions in making the pieces interlock with one another. Eventually, the puzzle is finished, matching the replica that guided them.

In the next chapter the puzzle will begin to take shape. We will discover that freedom from our false self is possible. In God's presence, we can be who we really are with the assurance that He knows us, loves us, and meets our deepest needs.

A Promise for Our Journey

Surely you desire truth in the inner parts;
you teach me wisdom in the inmost place.
—Ps. 51:6

CHAPTER 2
THE CHALLENGE OF SELF-DISCOVERY

As we toured the famous Rijksmuseum in Amsterdam, our tour guide told us that about 10 percent of Rembrandt's paintings were of himself. But far from being an exercise in self-aggrandizement, Rembrandt was a humble Christian who painted himself just as he was, with no embellishments. Artists have often wondered why he did not take advantage of his gifted hand and paint himself with just a touch of flattery since his physical form was far from handsome. But Rembrandt remarked, "Unless I can paint myself as I am, I cannot paint others as they are."

Until we are prepared to see ourselves for what we are in the light of the Scriptures, we will never be able to see others for what they are. Spiritual growth always involves a progressive knowledge of our own sinfulness, coupled with a deeper appreciation for God's grace. Someone has said that in heaven the biggest crown will not go to the biggest head. The hidden parts of the soul that we once thought were immune from inspection, even by God, become matters of concern when seen in the divine light.

FINDING OUT WHO WE ARE

If we try to find out who we are based on the messages given to us by our parents, friends, and associates, we will always be deceived because the pieces will not fit. Yes, their opinions are important, but they are also skewed. For one thing, their judgments are based on incomplete information. They know some things about us, such as our abilities, aptitude, personality, and the like, but they do not really know who we are inside. If we want to really know who we are we must discover this from someone who knows us "from the inside out."

Years ago a woman came to me for counseling because of a startling discovery: She returned home unexpectedly at midmorning only to see her husband dressed in women's underclothes prancing about the house. She'd been married for fourteen years and did not know that her husband was a transvestite! Throughout those years she was hardly qualified to reflect back to her husband who he really was! Yes, only an omniscient being, from whom we cannot hide, can really tell us who we are.

No human being is able to judge us by the right standard. Left to ourselves, we really don't know how to evaluate human behavior and motives. If we judge one person by another we can make some important distinctions, but we really cannot be sure whether our analysis is accurate. If I tell you, "You're okay," you have a right to ask, "By whose standard?" As teachers have discovered, their assessment of the troubled high-school teenager is quite different from that of his mother.

It is wrong to assume that just because we are well thought of, all is well. Some of the most dishonest people are those with spotless reputations. Like a tree whose shade is a blessing to those who pass by but whose trunk is filled with rot, these people deny that part of themselves that cries out for healing. They cannot be intimate and honest with others, for that would reveal a part of themselves that must be left concealed and untouched. If they were to begin to give and receive love, they would have to face pain they are determined to hide.

We can't find out who we are based on people's opinions because human judgments fluctuate. A man marries a woman and believes she is "wonderful," but two years later he meets someone who is even more "wonderful." His wife—bless her—has changed her opinion of her husband, too. The partners who at one time affirmed one another now hate each other. They have entirely different opinions about themselves and one another.

The opinion people have formed about you will determine what they see. If they perceive you as stingy, your generosity will be interpreted as an attempt to impress others; if they see you as deceptive, no actions you can take will change their conviction. In other words, the more settled their opinion of you, the more your actions will be interpreted through their prism. Sometimes no evidence will change their perception of you.

Actress Minnie Driver says that at the age of sixteen she was so desperate to get one boy's attention that she signed up to model in his art class so he'd be forced to look at her for hours at a time. But the plan backfired: He would mock her by drawing her with distorted features! So much for building our self-image on what others think!

People will "draw" us according to their liking. Our parents gave us one portrait, our friends another. Those who are famous have a different portrait drawn every day by those who love them and those who hate them, and they do not know whom to trust. If we base our self-worth on what others think about us, we will become addicted to approval.[1] Take that a step further and you can explain an exhibitionist who must do progressively more risqué things to attract continual attention.

At last we are able to give at least a partial answer to the question of why good people do bad things: As fallen creatures we deny that part of us we don't want to admit to, and we are committed to protecting our self-image, no matter the cost. Robert S. McGee wrote, "One of the tragic implications of this event [the Fall] is that man lost his secure status with God and began to struggle with feelings of arrogance, inadequacy, and despair, valuing the opinions of others more than the truth of God."[2]

So, to where do we turn to answer our original question: Who are we? Can we find a mirror that shows us who we really are? Yes, we can, and in the process we can be changed, freed from the need to deny who we are. All of us need a mirror that is more accurate—more revealing than our parents could ever be. We need a mirror that goes well beyond our physical image, beyond our well-constructed defense mechanisms; we need a mirror that reveals us for what we are and shows us what we can be.

GOD'S MIRROR

The Bible was written to help us with our one huge "blind spot." It tells us not only who we are, but also what God has done about it. When we open its pages we are struck with the two conflicting portraits of humankind: First, we marvel at man's greatness, for he alone among the creatures of the earth was created in the image of God. As we have already learned, his capacity for creativity, discovery, and generosity is endless. But, thanks to the Fall, so is his capacity for self-deception, deceit, and horrific evil. Pascal often spoke of this dual portrait: "He retains a faint desire for blessing, which is the legacy of his first nature. But he is plunged into the miseries of his blindness and lust, which has become his second nature."[3]

Recently, the lead item on a news radio program I was listening to reported that a man had strangled a disabled woman, throwing her body in an alley. The very next story was that of a woman who had pulled her SUV up to a children's home and unloaded cartloads of Christmas presents, only to leave without a trace. One member of the human race does evil, while another does good. The good person believes he needs no improvement; the bad one feels hopeless. Thus, as Luther pointed out, the natural man, like a pendulum, vacillates between pride and despair.

James says that the Bible is a mirror that won't allow us to manufacture a false portrait of ourselves. When we see ourselves in the light of its teachings, we will finally have a realistic reflection of who we really are and who we can become. Let's hear what he has to say:

> Do not merely listen to the word, and so deceive yourselves. Do
> what it says. Anyone who listens to the word but does not do what

it says is like a man who looks at his face in a mirror and, after looking at himself, goes away and immediately forgets what he looks
like. But the man who looks intently into the perfect law that gives
freedom, and continues to do this, not forgetting what he has heard,
but doing it—he will be blessed in what he does. (James 1:22–25)

The mirrors in those days were made of a mixture of copper and tin
and provided only an approximation of the reflection. When mission-
aries make contact with primitive people, they often give them a mirror
so they can see themselves. Just think, some people live their whole lives
knowing what others look like but not knowing what they themselves
look like!

Without an objective reference point, we cannot have an accurate
diagnosis; and without an accurate diagnosis, we will opt for the wrong
cure. We could say that God's Word is like an x-ray that probes deeply
into our hearts. We are like the girl who, when sweeping the room,
closed the blinds because the sunshine revealed the dust. When God
comes to us, He will pull up the shades so that we see the dust, but only
that He might clean the room. He has both a diagnosis and a cure.

If we resist exposure, if we come to the Scriptures with our minds
made up and our wills determined to do what we want to do, God's
Word will not change us. Open vulnerability is frightening, but unless
our hearts are open, the Word will penetrate no more deeply than water
on a marble slab. James says we will be only a "hearer" of the Word; that
is, we will be like an auditor who hears the words but will not respond
to the message. Never underestimate the deafness of those who do not
want to hear.

A man who was not fond of the opera, nevertheless attended with his
wife, and throughout the event he seemed to genuinely enjoy it. At times
he smiled, clasped his hands, and closed his eyes, and he did not complain about its length. When they were returning home, his wife compli-
mented him on his growing appreciation for music. But he explained
that, in point of fact, he was not listening to the opera at all but had

attached an earplug to a transistor radio in his pocket! His favorite base-ball team was in town, and this was the next best thing to attending the game! He's a reminder that even those who nod their heads affirmatively might be accepting only what is filtered through their psychological grids. The message you give is not the one they hear.

We must commit to honesty and basic integrity in reading and meditating on the Scriptures. The part of us that we withhold from others, and from God, is what blocks spiritual fulfillment and growth. If I have a secret life that is at war with my projected self, the more painful it will be for me to resolve my inner conflicts, and worse, I will displease the Lord. "He who conceals his sins does not prosper, but whoever confesses and renounces them finds mercy" (Prov. 28:13).

The Diagnosis of Our Need

As we stare into God's mirror we are startled by our own sinfulness. All human measurements must be cast aside when compared with the holi-ness of God. Here, finally, we understand why other estimates of us are so superficial. "The LORD does not look at the things man looks at. Man looks at the outward appearance, but the LORD looks at the heart" (1 Sam. 16:7).

Calvin was right when he said that it is impossible for us to know who we are until we know who God is. As long as we measure ourselves by our own yardstick, we might give ourselves a passing grade, but in the presence of God we all fall woefully short.

We discover that not only are we all sinners, but equally so. Of course there are some people who commit greater sins (and crimes) than oth-ers, and such distinctions are important. But in the presence of God such distinctions don't mean as much, "for all have sinned and fall short of the glory of God" (Rom. 3:23). Before Him we are on equal ground.

God, of course, has complete knowledge of us, including our motives, desires, and hidden sins. "Nothing in all creation is hidden from God's sight. Everything is uncovered and laid bare before the eyes of him to whom we must give account" (Heb. 4:13). This is terrifying, but it is also comforting. What a relief to know that in His presence, we no longer have to pretend. We finally have the courage to admit who we are, set aside our facade, and face our motives, desires, and lusts. At last we confess reality.

The Prescription of Grace

At this point Christianity differs from all other religions and secular psychological theories. The common understanding is this: We should think of ourselves as valuable simply because of who we are—unique people with the ability to create, to live in peace, and to love others. And, oh, yes, we should "love ourselves" regardless of what we have done, for we are inherently worthy.

Virtually all religions and philosophies teach moralism, the obligation we have to live decent lives following the rules of society. The emphasis is on duty for duty's sake and for the sake of others around us. But the problem is that we simply do not have the strength in ourselves to follow these rules, and what is more, we lack motivation to do so, especially if we can find a shortcut to satisfy our cravings. Our failure creates a sense of guilt, and if the self-condemnation becomes intolerable and the rules impossible to live up to, we jettison the rule book and do as we please.

Contrast this with the New Testament: For openers, it does not teach that we have special value in and of ourselves, much less that we should love ourselves in the usual sense of the word. Rather, the message is that our value is derived from the fact that we are loved by God. Luther was right: "God does not love us because we are valuable, but we are valuable because God loves us." We are valuable because we are objects of God's undeserved grace.

Grace changes our motivation; grace gives us the ability to take heart despite our struggles and our sins. Study the religions of the world and see if you can find anything that compares to the majestic promises of the New Testament.

How great is the love the Father has lavished on us, that we should be called children of God! And that is what we are! The reason the world does not know us is that it did not know him. Dear friends, now we are children of God, and what we will be has not yet been made known. But we know that when he appears, we shall be like him, for we shall see him as he is. Everyone who has this hope in him purifies himself, just as he is pure. (1 John 3:1–3)

Think of it this way: While other religions say we should love one another as a human virtue, Christianity says we should love one another because we have been loved. We should show mercy because we have been shown mercy; we should forgive those who have wronged us because we were forgiven by God. We are not working to become; we are working because we already *are!* As we shall learn, everything we are asked to do is based on what God has already done.

This is why conversion to Christ is critical. "Therefore, if anyone is in Christ, he is a new creation; the old has gone, the new has come!" (2 Cor. 5:17). There is a story of a painter who saw a beggar whose clothes were tattered, hair unkempt, and face dirty. The artist decided to paint the man as he might have looked if he had had the dignity of a job and a home. When he invited the beggar to see the painting, the beggar did not recognize himself. "That's me?" he asked. "Yes," said the painter, "that's what I see in you." For the first time in years the aging man was given hope, and he promised, "By God's grace, I'm going to be the kind of man you see me to be."

God paints a picture of us—quite different from the one we've painted of ourselves or others have painted of us. He begins by painting us as we are with all of our ugliness, self-condemnation, and insecurities that compel us to derive our sense of value from people or circumstances. Then He paints a second picture of us as sons and daughters, called as His beloved; He tells us that no matter how bad things get on earth we can look forward to a blessed future in His presence. He takes us out of the mud and tells us that we will walk on marble; He takes us from the pit and tells us that we are pardoned.

- To the abused child God says, "Let the little children come to me, and do not hinder them, for the kingdom of God belongs to such as these" (Mark 10:14).
- To the teenager fighting for acceptance among his peers, He says, "For you did not receive a spirit that makes you a slave again to fear, but you received the Spirit of sonship. And by him we cry, 'Abba, Father'" (Rom. 8:15).
- To the poor man cheated out of a decent life, He says, "He has filled the hungry with good things but has sent the rich away empty" (Luke 1:53).
- To the woman who has just lost her husband, He says, "The LORD watches over the alien and sustains the fatherless and the widow, but he frustrates the ways of the wicked" (Ps. 146:9).
- To those who are filled with self-condemnation, He says that He will wash us "whiter than snow" (Ps. 51:7).

In God's presence we admit our great need, and we are freed from the pressure of living up to the expectations of others. We are no longer devastated if some of our friends see us as less than our best. What our family and friends think about us is important, but not critical. Whether we have wealth, fame, or power is important, but not necessary for our contentment. We are liberated from the need to maintain our false self.

Somewhere I read a story about two underage boys accused of murdering a two-year-old boy. They strongly denied it, despite the evidence and the inconsistency of their stories. One was especially adamant, shouting, "I didn't do it!" Just then his mother wrapped her arms around him and said, "You are my son, and I promise to love you no matter what you have done." Immediately he broke into tears. "I did it, I did it," he admitted. Only unconditional love gives us a safe place, where we can confront the reality of who we are and what we have done. Grace guarantees that honest self-exposure will not destroy us. Grace gives us freedom to expose that unlovable part of ourselves, without fear that we will be rejected and irreparably harmed. Grace says that there can be no healing without honesty.

Should our friends speak evil against us—yes, even if we are slandered—we do not have to "even the score" because we know that all has not been told. Truth be known, we are far greater sinners than our enemies have made us out to be. If we suffer personal injustice, we will not be possessed with vindictiveness; and when tragedy comes, it will not destroy our security, for we have come to trust a God who knows us and cares for us. At last, we have a sense of identity and value that neither circumstances nor people can take from us.

Personally, I've learned that my identity is tangled up with how others perceive me. I have to keep relearning that although I am a pastor and an author, I am fundamentally a sinner learning to be content with God's presence and grace. And when the day comes when I have to leave my vocation, I am hoping that I will be satisfied just to be radically loved by God; I want to be one whose relationship with the Almighty is itself fulfilling. As Christians we have to keep reminding ourselves that our real identity is bound up with Christ and not with how others define us.

Our acceptance by God is not performance-based. We do not have to make ourselves better to receive His grace. It is impossible for us to make ourselves more worthy, for it was not our "worthiness" that made us attractive to Him. Grace cancels the need for worthiness; grace is the free gift given to those who believe. Since God's love assures us that we will never be disowned, it gives us the freedom to be honest, the freedom to look within and admit who we are, then accept His provision for our deficiencies in the common experiences and struggle of life.

Bonhoeffer was right when he said that only because we follow Jesus Christ can we be genuinely truthful, "for then he reveals to us our sin upon the cross. The cross is God's truth about us, and therefore it is the only power which can make us truthful. When we know the cross we are no longer afraid of the truth."[4]

THE TRANSFORMATION BEGINS

Remember Nathaniel Hawthorne's story "The Great Stone Face"? Some rocks on the side of a mountain had been thrown together in such a position as to resemble the features of a man. When the little boy, Ernest, inquired about the face, which was both noble and sweet, his mother told him that the village believed that someday a child would be born who would resemble the Great Stone Face.

Ernest never forgot the story. He spent every free moment gazing at the features across the valley and yearned for the day when the right man would come to the village. Many men appeared, but alas, they did not resemble the face in the valley. Ernest was disappointed, but he gazed at the face even more.

When he reached old age, he was thoughtful, generous, and kind. People came from afar to talk with him. One day when a poet came to the valley, Ernest believed that this man, whose poetry was so captivating, might be the fulfillment of the prophecy. But, again, it was not to be.

As Ernest addressed an audience gathered in the open air, the poet himself recognized that Ernest was the likeness of the Great Stone Face he had gazed at for so long. "But we all, with unveiled face *beholding as in a mirror the glory of the Lord,* are being transformed into the same image from glory to glory, just as from the Lord, the Spirit" (2 Cor. 3:18 NASB; emphasis added).

We become what we gaze at.

When we look in the mirrors around us, we may still be confused as to who we are. When we look into God's mirror and see both ourselves and His grace, we are changed by the Holy Spirit. That part of us that we hide, whether because of our sins or the hurts caused by those who have sinned against us, that part of us can be restored and healed. Our restless hearts are at peace with God.

After he was converted, the great theologian Augustine met his mistress with whom he had conceived a child. As she ran toward him, she shouted, "It is I!" To which he replied, "It is not I!" He was now a different person, no longer a slave to lust, having been changed by divine grace.

This would be a good place for us to stop and pray, to admit to God that part of us we have been hiding. To Him we bring our fears, our secret sins, and our deep hurts. We acknowledge that the fight is over; the anger, denial, and accusatory tone of our lives are now laid bare before the One who knows us completely and inhabits the most secret part of our being. At last, we know where we find rest. The open vulnerability that threatens us is the first step to freedom in Christ.

We have only begun to answer the question of why good people do bad things. Self-discovery has just begun. Keep reading.

A Promise to Ponder

Nothing in all creation is hidden from God's sight. Everything is uncovered and laid bare before the eyes of him to whom we must give an account. . . . Let us then approach the throne of grace with confidence, so that we may receive mercy and find grace to help us in the time of our need.

—HEB. 4:14, 16

CHAPTER 3
DECEIVED AND LOVING IT

GEORGE STEPHANOPOLOUS, who was an adviser to former President Clinton, wrote these words after the president's relationship with Monica Lewinski became international headlines: "The battle is all but over, and I'm still mystified by the Clinton Paradox: How could a president so intelligent, so compassionate, so public-spirited, and so conscious of his place in history act in such a stupid, selfish, and self-destructive manner?"[1]

Why do people who are otherwise so decent, smart, and well-intended—yes, even some committed Christians—behave in ways that are stupid, selfish, and self-destructive? And sometimes evil? Why don't we live up to what we know is right?

The answer, quite frankly, is that we are driven not by reason, but by our desires. We do not behave according to what our mind tells us; we obey our passions that cry out for gratification. To quote the words of Woody Allen (who fell in love with his own stepdaughter), "The heart wants what it wants."

This became clear to me when I began counseling people early in my pastoral ministry. I honestly believed that if I could show them rationally and biblically why a certain course of action was right, they would follow it. But time after time I realized that people wanted to do what they wanted to do, and reason did not (except in a few instances) carry much weight. Rationality, consistency, and long-term consequences had little impact on those who were determined to follow their heart wherever it led them. And if their heart was led astray, their mind was obligated to follow.

Listen to the words of Bob Pittman, chairman of MTV, that powerful video channel loaded with sexual messages intended to break down moral fences and any teenager's commitment to chastity: "The strongest appeal you can make . . . is emotional. If you can get their emotions going, forget their logic, you've got 'em. . . . We make you feel a certain way as opposed to you walking away with any particular knowledge. . . . It's the style not the substance."[2] He's right, of course: Get someone's emotions (i.e., desires) going, and logic will soon be forgotten. So will decency and moral responsibility.

A woman brought up in a Christian home married well. Her husband was a committed Christian; he taught Sunday school and was of service to his community in other ways as well. But she was bored with the marriage and felt that her deepest needs were not being met. She fell in love with a man in the neighborhood and left her husband and three children to pursue her dream. Of course, her illicit romance came to an inglorious end, so she pursued another man and then another. The surprise was not just that she became an adulteress, but that she did not even ask for custody of the children. Today her husband hardly recognizes her as the woman he married. What happened to this caring, committed, Christian woman? Would not she, given her upbringing and background, know that regardless of the inner pain, breaking God's rules for self-gratification would leave her more destitute than ever?

The New Testament writer James tells us that we cannot blame God for tempting us, "but each one is tempted when, by his own evil desire, he is dragged away and enticed" (1:14). *Dragged away by evil desires!* What a description of the human heart; what a reminder that evil desires can overtake us, and once we embark on our own path, returning to the starting point becomes well nigh impossible. How easy it is to choose what appears to be the easy path rather than the difficult but right one.

Freud, for all his errors, had a point when he said that within us there is a struggle for supremacy: Either the social restraints keep our aggressive drives under control, or these desires break out and result in unacceptable behavior. So we can be thankful for some cultural taboos that help restrain these inner warring drives. Laws have a similar function in keeping behavior in check. What Freud did not understand, of course, is that our desires can be changed by God (a topic to be considered in another chapter).

The purpose of this chapter is to take an in-depth look into the human heart, to understand the source and nature of our deceptions, and in the end, to agree with God when He says, "The heart is deceitful above all things and beyond cure. Who can understand it?" (Jer. 17:9). Our journey into the contours of human nature might make us uncomfortable, for we will be peering into our own hearts. But the better we understand our deceptions, the more thankful we will be for God's cure.

Our tour begins in the Garden of Eden, where the first deception occurred. We'll discover that we deceive ourselves because we want to be deceived: Yes, we are deceived and we love it. Thankfully, God does not leave us as He finds us but offers hope to all.

DECEIVED IN PARADISE

What surprises us is the environment in which Eve sinned! She herself was perfect; she did not have a sinful nature to lead her astray. Adam and Eve were created good, *innocent* in the truest sense, because they did not know the debilitating effects of sin. They had direct communication with God, and in the presence of one another, "they felt no shame" (Gen. 2:25).

Eve had no insecurities. She did not have to compete with supermodels whose pictures grace our newsstands. She did not have to keep her eye on the woman next-door who seemed to be all too friendly with her husband. In fact, she had a *perfect* husband. She did not have to complain about his laziness, for he was thoughtful and kind. She did not have to lie awake at night wondering whether she had married the right man!

Eve had a perfect environment with plenty to eat and was, by all accounts, culturally satisfied. God asked Adam to take care of the Garden, and since they were to rule together over all creation, she would help him take care of it.

Was she hungry? There was plenty to eat. Did she have a penchant for beauty? The flowers and trees of paradise would fulfill her every wish. Did she long for a harmonious marriage? With Adam she had no strife, no arguing. Did she want to be loved? She was loved by her husband and by God.

Today many psychologists accept behaviorism, that is, the notion that our behavior is largely determined by our environment or culture. People are not evil, we are told; society is. People steal because they are poor. They are immoral because culture tells them that having multiple partners is the route to happiness. They lie because cultural norms stand in the way of their happiness. Give people the right environment and they will be loving, selfless, and otherwise content.

Yes, I agree that sometimes people steal because they are poor; often cultural values contribute toward destructive behavior. But that is just part of the story. The other part is that even in the best environment, in the best neighborhoods, in the best climates, people still do evil things. Not all the criminals who have shot others in our high schools are from poor homes in the inner city. Affluent families in the suburbs often discover, to their horror, that their children are capable of evil, too. Criminals sometimes come from loving families who live in beautiful homes and have plenty to eat.

If you ask why Eve chose against God though she did not yet have sinful desires, I have no answer. In effect, this is the same problem we encounter when we think of the fall of Lucifer, who turned out to be Satan. We don't know why a perfect being, serving a perfect God, became discontented. We can only affirm that this happened. In the Genesis account we are simply confronted with the reality that a man and woman, created good by God, turned away from Him. And, most likely, we would have done the same.

Eve turned away from God's blessings to disobey Him. She committed her great sin in the face of great goodness. There were hundreds of trees that she could have eaten from; only one was forbidden. We're not even told that Adam and Eve were prohibited from eating of the tree of life; theoretically, they could have eaten and apparently been immortalized as righteous people. There was but one tree, the tree of the knowledge of good and evil, from which they were not to eat, "for when you eat of it you will surely die" (Gen. 2:17). Surrounded by untold privileges (this was paradise, remember), Eve turned away to do her own thing, to gain her own sense of independence.

Just so, some people do evil within the context of many blessings. Fine homes, vibrant churches, and praying relatives—all this does not prevent the possibility of a child following his untamed desires. We do not have to be raised in bad surroundings to do bad things; we just have to choose to gratify the "cravings of our sinful nature," as Paul put it (Eph. 2:3). The history of the human race proves this to be so.

What was the nature of Eve's deception? She depended on her natural perceptions, which distorted reality. She took a finite estimate of the situation, not realizing that her ability to assess the consequences of disobedience was limited. Rather than looking outside herself to God's special revelation, she looked within and chose to follow the lead of her curiosity. In the process, she tripped a series of dominoes with devastating eternal consequences.

Let's try to identify the deceptions so that we might understand ourselves better.

Perceptions, Not Instructions

We visualize Eve standing before the tree, comparing the warning of God with the promise of the serpent. "When the woman saw that the fruit of the tree was good for food and pleasing to the eye, and also desirable for gaining wisdom, she took some and ate it. She also gave some to her husband, who was with her, and he ate it" (Gen. 3:6).

Obviously, in and of itself the fruit was good, for all that God created was good. In one sense she was right when she saw that the tree was "good." There was nothing intrinsic in this tree that made it different from other trees.

God had, however, attached a penalty to eating it. Human sight cannot perceive the ultimate realities that lie behind our perceptions. God built in consequences for eating the fruit that were imperceptible to the human eye. To Eve, standing in the lush garden, looking at a tree that looked similar to the others, it appeared that God was wrong; His instructions were not in her best interests.

God called the tree the "tree of the knowledge of good and evil." But Eve gave it a different label. She saw it as good for the body (food), good for the soul (beautiful in appearance), and good for the mind (it would make her wise). So she felt free to eat. God called the eating of the tree *evil;* Eve called it *good.* She was a better judge of right and wrong than God. She preferred her perceptions to God's instructions!

This forbidden tree was "desirable." Her desires were more present to her than rational considerations. The passions of the body were given precedence over the needs of the soul. If she didn't eat of the tree, she would spend the rest of her life wondering what it would have been like to enter into the realm of the "knowledge of good and evil." So the serpent, in effect, told Eve, "*Feel,* don't think!"

Eve has many daughters. One young woman said that she accepted a man's invitation to go to bed with him because if she didn't, she would "always wonder what it would have been like." Curiosity is often the lure that leads us to set aside our better judgment. Sin never comes to us properly labeled; it always appears wrapped in a different package and presented as something other than what it is. The deadly hook is camouflaged with all kinds of appealing delicacies. If we follow our fallen nature, we will call evil good and good evil.

Just up the street from the Moody Church in Chicago is a pastor who performed the marriage ceremony of two homosexuals. Now, obviously, this is contrary to what the Bible teaches about homosexuality. But just as obviously, this pastor does not believe joining two males in marriage is a sin. He called the marriage "a holy union" and "an act of compassion and love." I have no doubt that he is as confident as Eve that his perception is correct and God's Word is wrong.

Eve, we are told, was deceived, but Adam ate knowing full well he was doing wrong (see 1 Tim. 2:14). Sometimes we are deceived like Eve; sometimes, like Adam, we choose sin with abandon, without the slightest doubt that we are turning away from God. Either way, few people who violate God's laws call it sin; most change the label to "loving" or "the best in this situation" or "a courageous act of authentication." We're deceived because we want to be.

A man who used pornography justified it with an argument reminiscent of Eve's: God created the human body and made it beautiful; thus, in admiring God's creation, we honor God. And, like Eve, he is quite right, except for one fact: God has attached a penalty to lust, and when we engage in it, there are consequences. Pornography defiles not only the user, but also those in the industry who are lured and exploited. Henry Rogers, speaking of this, writes, "Men don't want to see the pain and abuse behind the mask. They want to believe the deception."[3] Just like the fruit on the tree of Eden, pornography is not what it appears to be.

Our hearts deceive us by recruiting our minds to rationalize our behavior. Though we are capable of reason, we can become unreasonable the moment it appears as if our needs are not being met or if our individuality is threatened. When our desires call, reason becomes their slave, trying to find some way to obey their voice.

Like Adam, who was "willingly deceived," we are tempted to do a calculation: Will following my passions bring a happiness that will be greater than any distress my actions can bring? Of course, once we have started down that path, our passions will demand immediate gratification, and we will be blind to the consequences. Or, as has been said, we'll "sin today and deal with the devil tomorrow." What grieves God is that we are more comfortable with our sin in His presence than in the presence of others.

Eve teaches us that we cannot trust perceptions. For example, the sun appears to set, but in point of fact it does not; it is the rotation of the earth that causes sunsets, not the rotation of the sun. Things are not as they appear to us, but how they appear to God. His eternal perspective, not our limited knowledge, must be the basis for our actions.

The Serpent, Not God

For whatever reason, Eve thought that the serpent's revelation superseded the revelation of God. In her mind, the serpent represented a better, if not higher, authority. He had insight that either God didn't know or, more likely, God knew but wanted to keep from her. At any rate, the serpent's revelation appeared more accurate, more believable, and more likely to represent the true facts of the case. Best of all, his promise resonated with the desires of her heart.

Mark it well: From now on human desires would dictate not only morality, but also theology; particularly, the doctrine of God would be shaped according to man's liking. Theology would no longer be based on what God says about Himself, but on what mankind thinks He *should* say about Himself. God created man in His own image, and now mankind would return the favor. Those who follow their own ways would redefine God to be whatever they want Him to be.

Today the religion of the serpent, often referred to as the New Age religion, gains multitudes of adherents. Sin is not the problem, we are told, but rather ignorance. If only we knew that we are already gods, if only we realized our "inner potential," we would not be bogged down with human limitations. Thus, people are free to follow their desires wherever they might lead without fear of judgment. No wonder Paul predicted that "evil men and impostors will go from bad to worse, deceiving and being deceived" (2 Tim. 3:13).

Since Satan was the first being who asserted his own supposed right to independence from God, it follows that those who have bought into his philosophy belong to his spiritual heritage. Those who have crowned themselves Lord of their own destiny have substituted themselves for God and have written their own view of reality. From now on there would be two kingdoms in this world, and every human would belong to one or the other.

So, Eve did what she thought was best. Perhaps, since she was genuinely deceived, she thought that what was best was also right. If she had doubts, they were brushed aside. God, she thought, had no right to keep her from "fulfillment," but if He cared, He should affirm her every craving. There was a whole new world out there that she wanted to experience.

Time, Not Eternity

God had said, "When you eat of it, you will surely die." We don't know what Eve understood by this warning. She apparently could not grasp what death meant, since she had nothing in her experience to compare with it. Of this much we can be sure: She had no ability to predict the consequences of her actions.

Eve did not know that her sin would trip a series of dominoes that would plunge her offspring into centuries of suffering and endless pain. She did not foresee endless wars, greed and pain, and for millions an eternal hell. Standing there with her mouth watering for a taste of that luscious fruit, she couldn't have cared less about what tomorrow held. She did not know that she was sacrificing the permanent on the altar of the immediate.

How much better if Eve had decided to obey God's bare word, without needing further explanation! What if she had submitted her own desires to the commands of the Almighty, convinced that He knew more than she! What if she had trusted that God actually had in mind the best for her! Whether such obedience would have been possible (given the complexities of God's hidden purposes) is another matter. What is clear is that you and I are wise to obey Scripture whether or not we understand all the whys and the wherefores. We must never forget that there is a vast gap between the creature and the Creator.

When some Christian students went to the beach during spring break to witness for Jesus, they met a group of young men with six-packs of beer under their arms en route to a wet T-shirt contest. The Christian students—bless them—tried to present the gospel to the students, but it all seemed so absurd. Why should the revelers be troubled with God at that moment when the girls were waiting and the cold beer was in hand? "We'll deal with God later," was the impatient response. How could God compare with the present moment of excitement and passion? The present, not the future, mattered.

One summer my car was out of windshield fluid, so rather than drive to the store, I just added some water, which worked reasonably well. But one November morning here in Chicago, I used the washer only to see a film of ice quickly develop over my whole windshield! I had to pull off to the side of the road and scrape it off before I could continue. I learned that sometimes there is lag time between our behavior and its consequences! Sin, like a time capsule, has delayed action.

If you want to make a wise decision, ask: One thousand years from now, what decision will I wish I had made today? No decision can be good in time if it is not good in eternity. This explains why obedience to God is so essential today. He alone knows tomorrow; we deceive ourselves when we think that only today really matters.

What Satan wants us to do is to make such a heavy investment in the fulfillment of our desires that reversing our course seems impossible, perhaps even unthinkable. Whether it is the person who becomes immoral or the person who has been found drunk or the one who has begun to cheat—all of these sins and a dozen like them tend to become inflamed. Filled with self-condemnation, many of these people feel an inner compulsion to keep going in their fateful direction.

Why do good people do bad things? They follow the desires of the heart and turn away from the commands of Scripture. They substitute perceptions for instructions and their passions for obedience. In a word, they take the path of least resistance, following the dictates of their lower nature. Some people cross the line and become evil, willing to destroy those around them to justify their behavior. In a later chapter we will discuss that in more detail.

SEXUAL SELF-DECEPTIONS

The temptation of Adam and Eve was not sex. God had sanctioned marriage, affirming the nature of male and female. However, because sexuality lies at the heart of who we are and touches us so deeply, there is no matter about which we are as willingly deceived. The reason is simple: Since we are now tempted to define morality and even God by our desires, and since sexuality touches the most passionate part of our being, it stands to reason that here as nowhere else we will fight our greatest personal battles. We even put ourselves in the place of temptation, hoping to be tempted!

Sexual passions refuse to listen to the demands of rationality; they insist on immediate fulfillment, blotting out thoughts about the consequences. Only the present moment counts. A man whose affair had ruined his marriage told me, "I wanted to have this relationship and did not care about the cost. I thought it would work out, some way, somehow." Many who have said it could never happen must ruefully admit that they have fallen into sexual sin. Passions are more compelling than reason, refusing to heed the warnings along the road.

Since God's commands stand in opposition to our desires, we will either find reasons why He didn't mean it or argue that there is an exception for us. Or we might tell ourselves that the consequences of disobedience are manageable, since forgiveness has been promised to the repentant. A man tells himself that the reason he wants to have cable television is that he can get more sports channels, when the real reason is that he wants access to pornography. He lies to his wife, he lies to himself, and he lies to God.

"Do Not Be Deceived"

Paul warned against self-deception numerous times, particularly the temptation to let our passions dictate our beliefs. *"Do not be deceived:* Neither the sexually immoral nor idolaters nor adulterers nor male prostitutes nor homosexual offenders nor thieves nor the greedy nor drunkards nor slanderers nor swindlers will inherit the kingdom of God" (1 Cor. 6:9–10; emphasis added). Since it is true that the mind can rationalize anything that the desires dictate, we should not be surprised that many people blithely assume that they can rewrite God's commands to satisfy their every craving. They are deceived.

A young woman who moved in with a married man was warned by her parents, siblings, and friends that this was contrary to God's Word and that the eventual consequences would be bitter. Did she respond by saying, "Thanks for reminding me that this is wrong. Because I know that every mile I walk away from God, I'll have a mile to come back, and since I know that this relationship displeases God, I will break it off today, so that I can begin to honor God and be restored to my family"?

Don't you wish?

Of course that is not what she said. Her response to the warnings was, "My parents taught me the importance of love, and this is a loving, compassionate relationship. I'm sorry they feel this way, but I'm going with my heart because this is best for both of us." Her morality conforms not to God's revelation, but to her own desires and fantasies, and these *feelings* make her think even God approves.

There are two lessons that Eve's experience teaches us about deception: First, *Just because you can't foresee any consequences does not mean there won't be any!* God will not be mocked; unforeseen consequences will boomerang, often arising out of "nowhere." "Tell me the worst that can happen," a man contemplating adultery said to me. He believed that if he could manage the consequences, it might be worth the risk. He argued that his own marriage had grown loveless and now he had found a "soul mate" who met all of his needs, and by "God's good will," he met her needs, too. What the Bible defines as a "great sin" he now considers a "great act of love," an "act of becoming authentic." Evil is good and the good evil.

I think of a minister who claimed that he spent hours in prayer before he left his wife to live with a secretary with whom he had fallen in love. We might be tempted to think that he really didn't pray seriously about the matter, but I take his word that he did. There, mystically, in the presence of God, with an open Bible, he got the "peace" he had hoped for. If we want something bad enough, we will pray ourselves into a state of personal peace, so that we are free to do what we want. This "peace" will enable us to set aside the teaching of Scripture so that we can have our wish.

It would be impossible to calculate the number of affairs that have begun because one partner tried to help the other in his/her spiritual journey. In one renewal movement, where men counselors began praying with women and vice versa, relationships developed that led to sexual involvement. The reason is that our sexuality and spirituality are so closely united that spiritual intimacy can quickly lead to physical intimacy. Oneness of heart can quickly lead to a desire to complete the oneness and become one in body; and the spiritual dimension can make the physical relationship appear "sanctioned by God." As the relationship progresses, the couple blocks out all thought of future consequences, eager to believe the lies dictated by the deepest parts of their nature. This explains why pastors and counselors are particularly vulnerable to self-deception.

Sexual feelings are so powerful because we ascribe to them a sense of inevitability. "A common path to sexual sin," writes Louis McBurney, "is the notion that feelings are not only all-important, but also totally uncontrollable; they just happen to you."[4] We've often heard it said, "I did not intend to fall in love, but it just happened; suddenly we realized we were deeply in love." Some unfaithful marriage partners even deceive themselves by saying that they can still love their wives *and* this "other woman."

Love defies rational analysis. I often tell young people that they should remember it is possible to be madly in love with someone they should not marry. I've been told stories of how people have just met by "coincidence," and how this happenstance shows that their love was "meant to be." And yes, how this soul mate has awakened feelings within them that they did not even know were there, and how this shows that despite the odds, and despite the fact that no one seems to understand, they would be dishonest to deny the undying love they have for each other. The rationalizations are endless.

Forbidden Fruit

Two lesbians, both from Christian families, argued that their relationship was not only loving, but "beautiful." In fact, they were more certain that their relationship was honoring to God than they were about anything else. They had not yet learned the second bitter lesson Eve learned at such high cost to herself and to the human race: *Just because something is beautiful does not mean that it is right.*

Let me say it again: *Even beautiful fruit, if forbidden by God, incurs judgment.* There is no use arguing with an adulterer who has finally found someone who understands him, someone with whom there is communication, love, and oneness—there is no use arguing about whether the relationship is as beautiful as he says it is. The issue is not whether it is beautiful, but whether it is right; the question is not whether it is fulfilling, but whether God is pleased. It's not how we feel, but how we obey.

Lies used to justify various improper sexual conduct are legion. Dancers in strip clubs believe the lies of those who come to see them undress. One dancer said that her act was truly "beautiful" and "spiritual." They tell themselves that the compliments given by men are real, refusing to admit their crude manipulation. They live in a world of pain and abuse and yet try to portray a world of seduction and sexual fulfillment. They tell themselves that because they are beautiful, they have nothing to hide, when, in point of fact, they feel degraded and used. No matter how "beautiful," God has said no.

After Adam and Eve sinned, they hid in the Garden. They sewed fig leaves to clothe themselves, for they were ashamed (a topic to be discussed in Chapter 5). Here in Eden we have the beginning of defense mechanisms that will be used to control what other people think of us. Fallen man will become guilty of "doublethink," that is, the ability to believe two contradictory conclusions. He will feel guilty and yet give learned reasons why his actions are justified; though he will not have the motivation to be good, he will give the appearance of being good. He will fight any encroachment of light and in the process lie to himself, to others, and to God.

Surely, there must be an answer.

TOWARD THE PATH OF HOPE

A scorpion, being a very poor swimmer, asked a turtle to carry him on its back across the river. "Are you mad?" exclaimed the turtle. "You'll sting me while I'm swimming and I'll drown."

"My dear turtle," the scorpion said with a laugh, "if I were to sting you, you would drown and I'd go down with you. That would be contrary to reason."

"That's right!" cried the turtle. "Hop on."

The scorpion climbed on board and halfway across the river gave the turtle a mighty sting. As they both sank to the bottom, the turtle asked, "Why did you sting me? You said that was not reasonable. Why did you do it?"

"It had nothing to do with reason," the scorpion replied. "It's just my nature."

So, if it is a matter of nature, how can we have our natures changed? Since this will be considered at some length in a future chapter, I shall only mention here that God transforms the natures of those who come to Him for forgiveness and reconciliation. So much so that God's desires and ours should be one and the same. "Delight yourself in the LORD and he will give you the desires of your heart" (Ps. 37:4). In contrast, the desires of the wicked are evil (see Prov. 21:10).

How can we be kept from deceptions? God wants to provide continuity between the person I really am and the person you think me to be. Jesus chided the religious leaders of His day, "Isaiah was right when he prophesied about you hypocrites; as it is written: 'These people honor me with their lips, but their hearts are far from me'" (Mark 7:6). Some people have to get their twistedness untwisted so they no longer have to manage the discrepancy between head and heart.

Jesus wants the desires of our hearts and the praise of our lips to be united in the worship of God. What we sing in church and what we pray in our minds should be a reflection of our hearts. If we give money it is because we love God, if we serve it is because we love God, and if we tell others of His grace it is because we believe deeply in Him. Holiness is "wholeness."

"Sin always leads to hiding and to dishonesty," writes Jill Briscoe. "The devil laughs as he sees us with our shovels as the great cover-up begins."[5] We all remember the story of Achan, who stole what was the Lord's and then refused to admit what he had done until God helped Joshua pinpoint him and his family (see Josh. 7). Just so, we too are prone to hide what needs to be confessed and forsaken. God must often raise the level of our discomfort so that we are willing to "come clean," as the saying goes.

Honesty

First, we must be radically honest, willing to be kept from deception no matter the cost. This means not merely honesty in the presence of God, but also honesty in the presence of others. Listen to these words of instruction and warning: "See to it, brothers, that none of you has a sinful, unbelieving heart that turns away from the living God. But encourage one another daily, as long as it is called Today, *so that none of you may be hardened by sin's deceitfulness*" (Heb. 3:12–13; emphasis added).

Many of us handle what we believe to be the important matters of behavior and ignore the "little sins" that are tucked in our hearts. But it is precisely what we ignore that often become the seat of our problems; for small sins have a tendency to grow into greater ones. Sow a thought, reap a deed; sow a deed, reap a harvest.

One man put it this way. He said that he had a compartment in his mind that no one—not even God—was allowed to enter. Here, in this part of his being, he had room for lust, envy, fear, and insecurity. As long as the latch was closed and the walls sealed, he could enter whenever he wished and no one would know. But his heart could not be healed until he admitted that there was no place to hide. God loves to enter our safe places, to pry open the closets of our lives to assess our motives and delights. "Surely you desire truth in the inner parts; you teach me wisdom in the inmost place" (Ps. 51:6).

Follow the Word

Second, if we are sensitive to the Holy Spirit, God will convict us through His Word, which is His voice to us. One woman said that when her husband developed an attraction to another woman, though he was a pastor, he avoided Bible reading and prayer. It is difficult to even pretend to come into the light when we have something to hide. God wants the misery of our self-deception to be greater than the misery of self-examination and honest confession. He holds us accountable for not desiring Him above all else.

Which desire shall we follow? I'm reminded of the Indian who said, "I have two fighting dogs within me: a good one and a bad one." When asked which one wins, he replied, "The one I feed the most." Paul put it this way: *"Do not be deceived:* God cannot be mocked. A man reaps what he sows. The one who sows to please his sinful nature, from that nature will reap destruction; the one who sows to please the Spirit, from the Spirit will reap eternal life" (Gal. 6:7–8; emphasis added).

Not for a moment do I suggest that our battle with our passions will subside. The desires of our sensual nature will always conflict with our desire to please God. But we must grow a passion for Christ that is greater than our passion to sin. In fact, our willingness to know the truth lies at the heart of our discovery of it. "If anyone chooses to do God's will, he will find out whether my teaching comes from God or whether I speak on my own" (John 7:17). We often don't go looking for the truth for the same reason a thief doesn't go looking for a policeman. We are not looking for the truth with the same passion as we are looking for reasons to justify ourselves.

Joseph knew the power of sensual seduction. "Now Joseph was well-built and handsome, and after a while his master's wife took notice of Joseph and said, 'Come to bed with me!'" Joseph explained that the answer was no, since his master (her husband) trusted him and he could not betray this confidence. But Potiphar's wife was not that easily put off. We read that "though she spoke to Joseph day after day, he refused to go to bed with her or even be with her" (Gen. 39:10).

Imagine how easily Joseph could have rationalized the opportunity. For one thing the idea was not his, but hers; for another, they could make sure no one would find out—Potiphar himself had no suspicions, and Joseph's family was far away and had been out of touch for years. Furthermore, immorality was widely accepted in Egypt; there was no established ministry trying to maintain "family values." They could have a pack of lies ready in case someone questioned them. And those hormones, *day after day!*

So why did Joseph not tell himself that this was a God-given opportunity for fulfillment and that God would understand because after all, he was human? The answer is found in his reply: "How then could I do such a wicked thing and sin against God?" (v. 9). The affair could be hidden, the consequences could be controlled, and the relationship could be labeled "loving," but there was one fact that could not be ignored: This sexual relationship would offend the God Joseph had come to love and trust; He was watching, and that was all that mattered.

Note that Joseph did not relabel the sin to make it more acceptable.

He did not say, "How then could we have this affair?" or "How then could we have this 'beautiful, caring relationship'?" or again, "How then can I express my love with this soul mate?" He called it "such a wicked thing," and so it was. So instead of going to bed with a beautiful woman, Joseph went to jail without the assurance that he would ever be set free. Not until we call sexual indiscretions by the right name will we be kept from them. And not until we realize that our sin is against God will we be granted the grace to do what we should.

There is a story about a peasant who met St. Francis of Assisi. He asked, "Art thou Saint Francis?" To which St. Francis replied, "Yes."

"Take heed," said the peasant, "that thou be as good as men believe thee to be."

That is the wholeness for which we long; we want to be as good as people believe us to be. We don't want to deceive ourselves, others, or God. "My eyes will be on the faithful in the land, that they may dwell with me; he whose walk is blameless will minister to me" (Ps. 101:6).

A man who spent the better part of a year covering up his sin of adultery and murder and then finally confessed, wrote, "Blessed is the man whose sin the LORD does not count against him and in whose spirit is no deceit" (Ps. 32:2). Let us ask God to give us *a spirit that has no deceit!*

A Promise to Ponder

Then I acknowledged my sin to you and did not cover up my
iniquity. I said, "I will confess my transgressions to the LORD"—
and you forgave the guilt of my sin.

—Ps. 32:5

CHAPTER 4
THE PATH OF LEAST RESISTANCE

Richard Dortch, the television personality who was the friend and confidant of Jim Bakker back in the 1980s, wrote a book titled *Integrity: How I Lost It, and My Journey Back*.[1] Reverend Dortch has spent a great deal of time pondering a question: Why did he choose to conceal truth on the PTL television broadcast in order to defend Jim Bakker, knowing he was guilty? You might recall that Dortch got word that a certain Jessica Hahn confided that she had had sex with Jim Bakker in a motel room. In order to conceal the sad truth and to save the PTL ministry, Dortch arranged for "hush money" in a vain attempt to keep her from talking. But when the investigations began, the sordid truth was exposed, and both Dortch and Bakker spent time in jail.

Why did Dortch—a godly pastor and man of integrity—compromise his standards rather than expose the truth, no matter the cost? His reasons appeared noble enough: He wanted to save a great national ministry in which he believed. Against his better judgment, he compromised for the "greater good" of God's work.

Dortch failed, not because he was driven by his desires as such, but because he was driven by what he thought was a higher commitment. Though he abhorred deception, it was the path of least resistance. At the time, the path of truth appeared too steep to climb.

I've spoken to people who have entered the United States illegally. They are fine people, hardworking and lovers of freedom and, yes, truth.

But they faced a choice: Should they be honest and confess to the immigration authorities, or should they falsify information so they could remain here illegally? Yes, they loved the truth, but at times it is too costly. They settled for dishonesty, not because they wanted to, but because the alternative was too frightening.

I know a man whose vocation requires him to make multimillion-dollar deals for his company. He is a committed Christian; he wants to please God and leave a good spiritual legacy for his children. The problem is that occasionally his firm expects him to be dishonest, perhaps not blatantly, but dishonest nonetheless. This is the way the game is played, and if you play by strict rules of integrity, you will lose. So far, this man has acquiesced to the expectations of his bosses but wonders whether he can live with himself. He faces a crucial decision: What is of more value to him—the approval of God or a good job that enables him to provide for his wife and children?

I've just finished watching a one-hour television special on the Great Wall of China. I learned that the original wall, erected two hundred years before Christ, was built with dampened dirt that was firmly packed. But throughout the centuries it has eroded, and few traces of it remain today. In contrast, the later wall built with stones has not only been preserved, but will probably be standing as long as this earth remains. But, this stone wall was one hundred times more costly than the wall built with mud.

We face a choice: Do we take the cheaper route and build our lives on convenient decisions, or do we make the tough and right choices, at great personal cost? The world is so constituted that the right path is usually not the easiest path. History is replete with heroes who made huge sacrifices, sometimes not because they were forced to, but voluntarily. History also has many counterexamples of people who made a series of small compromises for themselves and served neither God nor man. Sometimes those for whom we have the greatest expectations bring us the greatest disappointment.

We have just uncovered another reason why good people do bad things: because the price of integrity and obedience is so high that compromise is more attractive. In other words, we are willing to violate our principles to achieve certain desirable ends. Some of those infractions can be minor, but at times we might be led to do some very bad things.

Of course, we have to get approval from our conscience before we cut corners and take the path of least resistance. We all long to be at peace, and if there is a part of our psyche that is out of sync, we will do all that we can to bring it in line with our behavior. Even in Nazi Germany the consciences of those who did evil had to be silenced. We are not guilty of their atrocities, but we all have different ways of "being at peace" with ourselves.

THE VOICE OF CONSCIENCE

Every one of us has a conscience that sits in judgment of all our actions. Now, it is true, of course, that not all consciences judge matters in the same way; thus, the Bible tells us that some have a weak conscience that can be trained (see 1 Cor. 8:7). Sometimes when I walk through the metal detectors at Chicago's O'Hare Airport, I set off the buzzer; at other times I do not. I've concluded that the difference might not be what I have on my person, but rather that sometimes the detector is more finely tuned.

Just so, my conscience might be set at one level and yours at another. In the early church, some people felt guilty for eating meat offered to idols and some did not (see Rom. 14). Your conscience might not be troubled by something that bothers me and vice versa. But of this much we can be sure: Everyone has a conscience; everyone knows the nagging sense of guilt for violating his/her moral codes. And because we dislike that persistent voice, we will do all we can to quiet it.

As we grow and mature, our conscience can either develop in the direction of sensitivity or deteriorate and become dead to the nagging of guilt or shame. If we violate it with impunity, it might no longer raise a voice in opposition to our actions and thoughts. A sociopath is one who is indifferent to morality and therefore can commit atrocities without a twinge of conscience. On the Web site of Eric Harris, one of the Columbine gunmen, these words were found: "God, I can't wait till I kill you people. Feel no remorse, no sense of shame. . . . All I want to do is kill and injure as many of you as I can."[2] What surprises us is that a conscience can be deadened at such a young age.

We might wonder how someone like the Oklahoma City bomber Timothy McVeigh is able to kill 168 innocent people and yet die without remorse. Such criminals have a disconnect between what they have done and what they will allow their conscience to feel. This disassociation allows them to live in two separate compartments, insulated from feelings, morality, and other people's pain.

To some extent, what is true of McVeigh can also be true of many people who appear to live lives beyond reproach. In world A, a man might be a deacon, meticulous in his conduct, serving diligently in the church, obsessed with how he appears in the presence of others. In world B, he can be molesting his daughter or having an affair, but he can look you in the eye and tell a lie without flinching.

Will versus Conscience

Whenever the will does not submit to the demands of the conscience, the conscience will be desensitized. And, a person who wishes to violate his conscience through deceit, anger, and a dogged commitment to evil will get his wish; his conscience will eventually be silenced. Paul shows that such a transformation is rooted in demonic activity. "The Spirit clearly says that in later times some will abandon the faith and follow deceiving spirits and things taught by demons. Such teachings come through hypocritical liars, *whose consciences have been seared as with a hot iron*" (1 Tim. 4:1–2; emphasis added). Man and the devil evidently can share this common trait: They can do evil without remorse.

It is interesting to see how often people will violate their conscience and for what price. In the book *The Day America Told the Truth*, James Patterson and Peter Kim give compelling evidence that the human heart is filled with deceit, that however much people say they love the truth, they will compromise it for some perceived higher personal good. And if we do not lie outright, we shape the truth to make us look good and protect our vaunted ego. They write, "Lying has become an integral part of the American culture, a trait of the American character. We lie and don't even think about it. We lie for no reason . . . and the people we lie to are those closest to us."[3] In fact, 91 percent of Americans lie regularly.[4]

Here are some sobering revelations about lying, deceit, and values. What would Americans do for ten million dollars?

- Twenty-five percent would abandon all of their friends, or church.
- Twenty-three percent would become prostitutes for a week.
- Sixteen percent would leave their spouses.
- Seven percent would kill a stranger.
- Three percent would put their children up for adoption.[5]

If some people are willing to sacrifice those who are most valuable to them for the sake of raw greed, we can be sure that millions of others are willing to commit the lesser sins of lying and stealing for immediate gratification. In either case, they will have to live with themselves, enjoying the "benefits" of their schemes but also struggling to stifle the persistent voice that tells them they have violated their own sense of decency.

What all this research reveals is that even those who claim to value truth, love, and integrity will sacrifice these values "if the price is right." They will opt for what appears to be most conducive to their own exaltation and base desires. The shortest path to happiness, as they define it, is to override the conscience and do what seems convenient for personal, narcissistic (i.e., selfish) gratification.

Not money, but peer pressure, is another reason why some people will turn a deaf ear to the voice of conscience. A teenage girl said, "I started smoking, not because I liked it—I hated the bits of tobacco on my tongue—but it is the price I have to pay to be one of the gang." And to be one of the gang, many her age have participated in everything from drug use to murder. We want to be accepted by those whose opinions matter; and if our friends matter to us more than family or God, we will do whatever it takes for acceptance, conscience notwithstanding.

This is why Proverbs warns, "My son, if sinners entice you, do not give in to them. If they say, 'Come along with us; let's lie in wait for someone's blood, let's waylay some harmless soul' . . . my son, do not go along with them, do not set foot on their paths; for their feet rush into sin" (1:10–11, 15–16). Many a fine son or daughter has been drawn into evil because he or she joined the wrong crowd, setting aside better judgment to listen to the voice of friends rather than to the voice of Scripture.

The reason the Bible warns against taking personal vengeance against those who have wronged us is not only because it shows lack of faith in God's justice, but also because we might violate our consciences when we "even the score." Paul warned, "Do not repay anyone evil for evil. Be careful to do what is right in the eyes of everybody. . . . Do not take revenge, my friends, but leave room for God's wrath, for it is written: 'It is mine to avenge; I will repay,' says the Lord" (Rom. 12:17, 19). When we become impatient with God's justice, we are tempted to overreact and do what we might regret.

In all these instances, the person sees his actions as a shortcut to happiness. To obey his better instincts simply seems too difficult. He is weary of swimming upstream and believes that life owes him the pleasure of the shortcut. This explains why 42 percent of Americans do not stand up for what they believe.[6]

RATIONALIZATIONS WE HAVE KNOWN

Let us never underestimate the ingenuity of human beings who are bent on avoiding the light of God's Word, or even the light of conscience. Jesus said, "This is the verdict: Light has come into the world, but men loved darkness instead of light because their deeds were evil. Everyone who does evil hates the light, and will not come into the light for fear that his deeds will be exposed. But whoever lives by the truth comes into the light, so that it may be seen plainly that what he has done has been done through God" (John 3:19–21). By nature we love the darkness because it is consistent with our deeds. Thus we are prone to self-deception and enshroud ourselves in a shield of denial, so that we no longer want to know the truth about ourselves. *We can deny anything we don't want to believe.*

If we are committed to walking in darkness, we will try to convince ourselves that the darkness is, in fact, light. The more sophisticated we become, the more sure we are that those who write their own rules are "enlightened." As we have already learned, the mind is now enlisted to negotiate a truce with that part of us that says, "You are not doing what you know is wrong." Here are some of the more popular rationalizations we use to justify taking the path of least resistance.

Rationalization #1: "Everyone Is Doing It"

Yes, our first line of defense is to say that "everyone is doing it—and if not everyone, at least enough others are doing it that I, too, have a right to do it." According to *The Day America Told the Truth,* "this rationalization has begun to take hold in all areas of our lives." One man said he rationalized stealing from his company because they were unfair to him. "If they can do it, I can do it too." Sixty-four percent of those ages eighteen to twenty-four have told themselves, "Everybody is doing it" and then have done something immoral.[7]

Nowhere is this rationalization seen more clearly than in sexual mores or the message of MTV. Anyone who has ever raised a teenager has heard the refrain, "All the kids at school do it!" Usually it is said with such defiance that only someone who was totally out of touch with reality could oppose it. If everyone does it, by definition it becomes right!

Rationalization #2: "It's No Big Deal"

Since we live in a culture that has no objective standard, who is to say what is right or wrong? And, if I compromise my principles, it is not really that serious. An administrator from the East Coast wasn't bothered about cheating on a final exam. "I had a copy of the exam with the answers in my hand when I took it. Does it matter? Do exams really matter?"[8] In other words, is cheating really that big a deal?

Rationalization # 3: "I'm Really a Good Person"

Incredibly, although most Americans lie every day and speak candidly about cheating and hidden sexual dalliances, the large majority believe that they are basically good people. Many people silence their consciences by telling themselves that the evil they have done is small in comparison to the good they have accomplished. They point to money given to charities, to love of family and friends, and to their sincere worship of God. They try to distance themselves from the bad they've done by thinking that this behavior is an anomaly, something that is not characteristic of their basic nature.

Drug lords have been known to help the poor in their community, Mafia members are often especially kind to their families; even criminals have a code of honor among themselves. In their minds, the good they do outweighs the bad and proves that they are not really bad after all. To illustrate its extreme form, I can do no better than to quote the words of a serial murderer who said, "It is not the people I have killed, but the ones I love and care about, that shows who I am."

Rationalization #4: "I Can Control the Consequences"

Most people honestly believe that they are crafty enough both to limit their own corrupt behavior and to limit (or eliminate) the negative fallout from their actions. They look at others who have traveled the same path and regard them as foolish for ending in ruin. Unfortunately, sin has a way of spinning out of control. It does not follow neat laws of cause and effect but often has consequences well beyond the limits we prescribe.

Who can calculate the number of sexual relationships, cases of fraud in business dealings, and personal lies that all began with the express intention of controlling the outcome? Millions have learned that the consequences of sin cannot be nicely quarantined. Because it is almost impossible to tell only one lie, another lie must be told to cover the first one. Thus, there develops an ever-widening circle of deception. And, in the end, God exposes whomever He wishes to expose. "If you fail to do this [follow the Lord], you will be sinning against the LORD; and you may be sure that your sin will find you out" (Num. 32:23).

Rationalization #5: "I Deserve This"

This is the argument of entitlement, the feeling that it is "my turn" to get a break from the tedious and unfair events of life. This is the "I deserve some happiness" syndrome that has become so much a part of our culture. At a time when greed is celebrated as a virtue, it should come as no surprise that people believe their personal gratification is their number one (and perhaps only) goal in life. Asked what he would want most, a male truckdriver answered, "I would like to be treated like a king and have a harem of women to do with as I please."[9] For many the philosophy is: "If I am not getting what I deserve, I will simply take it, no matter what."

Most people believe that there is an irreconcilable conflict between what is right and what brings the most happiness. Caught between their conscience on the one hand and their penchant for self-serving pleasure on the other, the scales are often tipped in favor of taking the shortcut. Such compromise means that they cannot say with Paul that they have a conscience that was free from offense before God and man.

Rationalization # 6: "If Things Go Bad, I've Got an Escape"

There are times when the voice of conscience cannot be silenced. Rationalizations, excuses, and time refuse to numb the hidden part of the soul. Lady Macbeth, an accomplice in the death of King Duncan, thought her bloodstained hands could be washed clean easily. "A little water clears us of this deed," she assured her husband.

Unconvinced, he intoned, "Will all the great Neptune's oceans wash this blood clean from my hand?" He answers his own question: "No. Rather, my hand shall make all the oceans bloody!"[10]

Lady Macbeth's conscience would not be stilled. "Here's the smell of blood still; all the perfumes of Arabia will not sweeten this little hand." Since the torture was unbearable, she did what twenty-five thousand Americans do every year—she committed suicide.

Perhaps if she had lived today she would have used alcohol and drugs to numb the conscience so that it would no longer bring trouble to the soul. Some people become compulsive in their work habits, refusing rest, so that they do not have to face the emptiness of a restless conscience. Whatever it takes, the conscience cannot be ignored.

I once owned a digital alarm clock that, for some reason, beeped every hour on the hour. I tried to shut it off, but apparently I could not properly manipulate the controls (I am technologically challenged!). As the weeks passed, I noticed that the beep was growing fainter, and eventually when the battery died, it ended all together. We should not be surprised that some people can commit crimes without remorse, for the last "beep" of their conscience has died out. In its place is an empty numbness, a sense of hopeless despair in which nothing matters anymore. When self-loathing sets in, anything is possible.

When Heinrich Himmler, the head of Hitler's SS troops, took over his responsibilities, he was faced with the question of how to deaden the consciences of decent young German men so that they would be willing to perform ghastly deeds of cruelty. Both Himmler and Hitler believed that this could be done only if each of the troops was forced to do an evil deed that would violate his conscience and sense of decency. Only when they did what others considered reprehensible would they break away from their own values.

The conscience was deadened through these acts of barbarism; these actions served the dual purpose of cutting the recruit off from past ties, family, and friends and bonding him to new peers and the new leader. The break would be so complete that he could never go back. An act of torture or a murder would unite him with fellow troops who had crossed the same line, felt the same numbness, and sworn to uphold the same cause.

Some of the recruits recoiled at killing a child or participating in the deliberate starvation of the Jews. To overcome this resistance, the Nazi leaders stressed that: (1) the men must fit in with the *gemeinschaft* (the community or the assembly) and do what all the other elite troops were doing, and (2) they must realize that cruelty is necessary for the greater good of a revived and prosperous Germany. Kindness and integrity were expected in family relationships but would hardly do in promoting the expansion of the Reich. Few troops refused orders, unwilling to risk the penalties disobedience would bring. Faced with the prospect of being ostracized or put to death, most took the path of least resistance.

No longer blessed with the gift of guilt, the voice of conscience grew silent and they were free to do evil. When the Lord visited the Tower of Babel, built in defiance of His instructions, He said that if they did this, "nothing they plan to do will be impossible for them" (Gen. 11:6). Read your daily newspaper and ask: Are there any limits to human wickedness, once people turn away from God?

REFUSING THE SHORTCUT

Moses is an outstanding example of someone who took the hard, but right, path. He chose scorn rather than honor and poverty rather than wealth; he chose servanthood rather than kingship. "By faith Moses, when he had grown up, refused to be known as the son of Pharaoh's daughter. He chose to be mistreated along with the people of God rather than to enjoy the pleasures of sin for a short time. He regarded disgrace for the sake of Christ as of greater value than the treasures of Egypt, because he was looking ahead to his reward" (Heb. 11:24–26).

Jesus did not enjoy the Cross, nor was He pleased with His assignment. Paul used Him as an example for us: "We who are strong ought to bear with the failings of the weak and not to please ourselves. Each of us should please his neighbor for his good, to build him up. *For even Christ did not please himself* but, as it is written: 'The insults of those who insult you have fallen on me'" (Rom. 15:1–3; emphasis added).

Like us, Jesus had conflicting emotions. There was a part of Him that did not want to go to the Cross with its humiliation and pain. No wonder He prayed, "My Father, if it is possible, may this cup be taken from me. Yet not as I will, but as you will" (Matt. 26:39). Thankfully, His resolute will was not deterred by His changing emotions, but He "set his face to go to Jerusalem" (Luke 9:51 KJV) and stayed there till His work was done.

Theoretically, He could have taken the shortcut. "Do you think I cannot call on my Father, and he will at once put at my disposal more than twelve legions of angels? But how then would the Scriptures be fulfilled that say it must happen in this way?" (Matt. 26:53–54). Given the reception He received as the Son of God, we would understand if He had said, "I have had enough" and called His armies to the rescue.

He knew that the way to the crown was the Cross, so He submitted to the Father's will. He refused to be duped by His human emotions or the momentary elation of bypassing the pain He came to endure. He had to look at the Cross from the standpoint of eternity, not time. Omar Bradley wrote, "We need to learn to set our course by the stars, not by the lights of every passing ship."

LIFE-CHANGING LESSONS

Daily we are confronted with choices, some seemingly insignificant, others with long-term implications. Sometimes we feel "boxed in," wanting to do what is right but enamored by the lure of the immediate. Alternatives to doing what is right are always easy to come by; substitutes are everywhere.

Here are some guidelines that challenge my thinking whenever I am tempted to take the easy path. "Endure hardship with us like a good soldier of Christ Jesus" (2 Tim. 2:3).

1. *When faced with a fork in the road, don't assume that the easiest*

path is God's will. A youth pastor, facing mounting credit-card debt, decided to use some of the money from his church budget to pay off his credit cards. He was a good man with good intentions of paying it all back; this was just an intermediate plan to cut back on the high interest rates. He saw this as the "Lord's provision" so that his wife would not have to know the extent of their debts.

But a few months later the deficit in the church budget was discovered, and no, he had not been able to make any payments back to the church. Though the leadership knew of his good intentions, they could not condone the secrecy and thievery. The path that looked so convenient turned out to be the path that led to his dismissal.

2. *We usually embark on the path of least resistance in small incremental steps, not big jumps.* When my wife and I left Vancouver for an Alaskan cruise, the ship pulled away so slowly we hardly noticed it until we were miles from shore. Just so, many lives have been ruined, not by big decisions to do wrong, but by small, incremental choices that seemed quite harmless at the time.

Richard Dortch asks, "Did I deliberately set out to become involved in fraud or deceit? Absolutely not, but when you get permission from your conscience to have a small secret then you get the green light to have an even larger secret. And that can be devastating."[11] But one lie led to being entangled in a web of deceit from which it was impossible to extricate himself. One small step in the wrong direction led to other, larger transgressions. Thus a good man can end up doing things that he never dreamed possible.

3. *Most people change not when they see the light, but when they feel the heat.* We will stay on the path of least resistance until we are forced by either circumstances or conviction to mend our ways. Of course, it is much better to change the trajectory of our lives because of an inner conviction than because of circumstances. But either way, human nature does not change easily. We might be open-minded to new ideas, but we are closed-minded when it comes to changing our cherished lifestyle. Just ask an alcoholic.

A Christian man formed an organization that paid interest to investors and lent out the money to others for a higher rate of interest. The problem was that many of the loans went bad because the lenders were not living up to their agreements. Yet the man continued to solicit new investors, knowing full well that he would be unable to repay them; any new money was used to cover current withdrawals. Not until the scheme came entirely unraveled did the truth surface, and dozens lost their investments.

Why didn't he end this scandal immediately when he realized he was headed for disaster? The answer is that we so fear exposure that we would rather dig ourselves a deeper hole if we can postpone judgment day by a week, a month, or a year. We will stay on the path of *least* resistance until it becomes the path of *most* resistance.

4. *We should never sacrifice the permanent on the altar of the immediate.* We've learned that people like Moses and Jesus made their courageous decisions to please God because they took the long-range view of life. Such decisions are based on eternal values.

There is a story about a young man who visited with William Gladstone, a prime minister of England in the mid- to late 1800s.

"What do you plan to do with your life?" the prime minister asked.

"I would like to get a good education."

"That's wonderful, but what then?"

"I would like to be elected to Parliament to make a difference in the quality of life in Britain."

"That's good, but what then?"

"I would like to write books to pass on what I've learned to future generations."

"That's good, but what then?"

"I guess I will have to die."

"That's true, and *what then?*"

"I've not given that much thought."

To which Gladstone replied, "Young man, get on your knees and stay there, *until you have thought life through to the very end.*"

Only those who have taken the long-range view of life will take the right path, not just the easy one. Only those who fear God more than man will put principle above privilege and obedience above comfort. The reward is satisfaction in this life and blessing in the next. Let us determine with Paul, "So I strive always to keep my conscience clear before God and man" (Acts 24:16).

Are we up to the challenge?

A Promise to Ponder

He whose walk is blameless and who does what is righteous,

who speaks the truth from his heart and has no slander on his tongue,

who does his neighbor no wrong and casts no slur on his fellowman

. . . . He who does these things will never be shaken.

—Ps. 15:2–3, 5B

CHAPTER 5
THE CURSE AND CURE FOR SHAME

Even if we can't define the word *shame*, we all know the feeling. We've all done some things that, if they were known, would cause us to be ashamed.

Shame is that sense that we have radically disappointed ourselves, others, and most of all, God. Shame can be defined as a painful emotion or sense of reproach or embarrassment that arises because of what we have done or because of what others have done to us. Shame tells us not merely that we have done wrong, but that we fundamentally *are* wrong; we are flawed, perhaps fatally.

Shame was not a part of the original creation, for we read, "The man and his wife were both naked, and they felt no shame" (Gen. 2:25). Imagine being psychologically transparent, with nothing to hide. No insecurities, no greedy aspirations, no lusts. No fear that one's spouse or God would be displeased if all the thoughts of the heart were revealed. Adam and Eve could be as transparent as glass, with no dread that they would be found defective.

Imagine—if you are a man—being so pure in thought, word, and deed that your wife, your sister, or your mother could know all your thoughts and you would have no fear of risking their displeasure. If you are a woman, imagine that your deepest cravings would be so holy that they could be thoroughly known to your husband and friends without embarrassment. Everything you think or do could be gloriously known, with the assurance that nothing revealed would change the unconditional love of others and God. No need to hide, no desire to hide.

Sin changed all that. After Adam and Eve sinned, they did have a deeper level of moral consciousness, just as the serpent had promised. But unlike God, their knowledge of evil was experiential; they would personally know its effects in their lives and the lives of their children. Now they are in anarchy, with God as a rival who must be defied.

Yes, they would "be like God" in the sense that they would assert their independence. They would rule themselves, acting as if they were little "gods" trying to take charge of their lives. Sin, which is defiance of God, would always have a special lure, and as we have learned, its desires would replace the commands of God.

Narcissism

With the Fall, narcissism was born. You might remember that Narcissus was the son of the river god Cephisus in ancient Greek mythology. He was a handsome youth, proud of his own beauty. Many girls loved him, but he paid no attention to them. The gods, the legend goes, were angry and punished him by making him fall in love with his own reflection in a pool of clear water. He was so much in love with himself that he could not leave the pool and was incapable of loving anyone else.

Whether we admit it or not, we are born in love with ourselves; we are born as gods of our own lives firmly planted at the center of our own universes. Because I am the center of my universe, and you are at the center of yours, we will constantly intersect and our sphere of influences will collide. When our selfish, individual worlds bump into each other, there will be conflict, arguments, and numerous subtle battles for supremacy.

Our narcissistic natures say, "If you show yourself to be better than I am, I will sustain narcissistic injury and will consider you an enemy. If you have more than I, I will be jealous of you; if you are more attractive than I, I will resent you; if you take what is mine, I will fight you. If I find you a threat to who I perceive myself to be, I will destroy you with lies and manipulation. I will try to get you to see life from my viewpoint and make your life impossible if you don't. A house will not be big enough for both of us; indeed, a neighborhood might not be big enough." No wonder the world is often at war!

The truly narcissistic person will interpret every event in relationship to himself, asking two questions: (1) How does this event make *me* look? and (2) How does it make *me* feel? If you say, "I like the cake Mrs. Jones baked," the response of the narcissist will be, "Well, don't you like *my* baking? What's wrong with what *I* bake? Answer me!" If a marriage partner says, "I have to stay late at work tonight," a narcissistic partner will interpret it as a personal threat: "You really don't want to be with *me*, do you?" As she came to his bedside, the first question of a narcissistic wife whose husband was taken to the hospital with a heart attack was, "How much life insurance do you have?"

News that someone has been caught in a scandal is greeted by the narcissist without sympathy and with no evident fear that he is vulnerable to the same sins. Rather, the narcissist sees the failure as an opportunity for self-exaltation and will probably comment, "*I* would never do that." There is a secret delight when others fail, for it makes the narcissist feel a notch better. In fact, lies, innuendo, and character assassination are used to undercut those whom the narcissist sees as a personal threat. The extreme narcissist believes that whatever evil he imagines about others is true. There is no court of appeal. Incredibly, *the same mind that manufactures lies actually believes them!*

There are animals who emit a strong odor to ward off predators, but they themselves are not debilitated by it. For example, the skunk, as far as we know, might think that his stench smells like a fresh bottle of Chanel No. 5. Just so, the narcissist is not aware that he is deeply hurting those around him. Unable to feel the pain of others, he is totally self-absorbed, believing that he is just fine, thank you. When confronted by his lack of compassion, he is genuinely puzzled and becomes defensive, points to his accomplishments, and denigrates those around him. He comes out smelling, well, like a rose. Narcissists believe that the world owes them a living simply by virtue of the fact that they were born on this planet.

I've heard a story about four men who were attending a large medical conference and always monopolizing the microphone, asking questions. Before the last session, the lecturer said, "If you have already asked questions, I request that you let others have the opportunity." But the same men disregarded his remarks and again used up all the time with their own comments and questions. An observer, leaving a meeting, said to a friend, "How could they monopolize the time after being told to let others ask questions?" To which his partner replied, "You must understand that *for narcissists there are no others.*"

Strictly speaking, of course, others do exist for the narcissist, but only as objects to be used. On the one hand he has no sympathy for others and is unwilling to expend himself for their needs, but on the other hand, the narcissist pursues and manipulates others to get admiration and approval. Thomas Merton rightly declared, "To consider persons and events and situations only in light of their effect on myself, is to live on the doorstep of hell."[1] It is from this hell that Christ has come to redeem us.

THE STIRRINGS OF SHAME

After Adam and Eve sinned, they hid themselves among the trees of the Garden; they who had felt no shame now felt its powerful impact. The trees, which had been given to them as a mirror through which they could see the Creator, now became a wall to hide themselves from Him and from one another. From now on, they would expend much psychological energy and ingenuity to keep hiding.

Adam and Eve now had reason to feel ashamed. God Himself gave them animal skins so that they could be properly covered (see Gen. 3:21). Their instinct was sound; there was no way back to Eden, no way back to innocence.

I read a story about a man who wanted to be totally open, to hide nothing. If you met him, he might say, "Your breath is a bit off," or he might tell a woman to whom he was speaking that he was lusting for her. He also joined a nudist colony, arguing that if he was naked physically, he could also be nakedly open psychologically. This, he insisted, was the way back to innocence, the way back to paradise where there is nothing to hide.

But there is no return to paradise. Dr. Donald Carson warns that there are some Christians who advocate a kind of spiritual nudism; they want to let all their dirty laundry hang out, believing in total psychological and spiritual transparency. But some things should not be talked about in public; they should remain hidden. We don't have to reveal our private thoughts to everyone. Certain sins have to be exposed, but love covers a multitude of sins.

Personally, I'm glad that my thoughts are hidden; I would not want you to know everything I think. And in return I'm glad I don't know all the things you are thinking. This is not to say that honesty is unimportant; indeed, it is basic to all self-discovery and spiritual growth. But honesty does not require that I reveal everything to everyone. God, of course, knows all things about me, but it is not necessary that human beings know every detail. As a general principle, my confession should be as broad as the offense. I confess only to those whom my sin has affected.

Adam and Eve were not trying to find their way back to God, but were hiding from Him. He initiated the search, walking in the Garden and calling out to the distraught couple. If anything, they were seeking to become their own gods so that they would not be exposed to the holiness of the Almighty whom they had wronged. But thankfully, the true God would not let them go. This search was the beginning of grace.

Shame now meant that the human race would be preoccupied with appearance. Clothing would not just be judged by whether it was warm or comfortable, but by how it appeared to others. Whether your fig leaves were as beautiful as mine would become a preoccupation, especially in rich cultures. What parts of the body should be hidden, and what parts exposed, would occupy the minds and hearts of the human race.

And the human body would be sculptured to make sure it appeared attractive. Exercise would be necessary, not just to remain healthy, but to have one's body toned, with all the right curves and shapes. Some young women would be so ashamed of their bodies that they would starve themselves to death, fearing that they were overweight. (Since eating disorders are also a control issue, they will be discussed in a future chapter.) We as humans would judge each other primarily by our appearance; thus, being "attractive" would become an obsession.

The Blame Game

Next, Adam and Eve began the blame game. They both admitted to what they had done, but they did not take responsibility for it: As the saying goes, the man blames the woman, the woman blames the serpent, and the serpent doesn't have a leg to stand on! From now on, man would stoutly resist owning up to his own responsibility. He would blame others, shape the facts to fit his ego, and if necessary destroy those around him in order to preserve his own sense of ownership and self-worth.

Albert Camus wrote in *The Fall*, "Each of us insists on being innocent at all cost, even if he has to accuse the whole human race and heaven itself."[2] Some people, filled with narcissistic obsessions, will be psychologically incapable of taking blame for anything, no matter how unjust, calloused, or abusive their behavior. They will also appear to be incapable of entering into the pain of others but will interpret such misfortunes only in relationship to themselves. They will go to their graves without uttering the words "I have sinned."

We can imagine the argument Adam and Eve must have had that evening.

Adam speaks first.

"Why did you eat that fruit? Didn't God clearly tell us that we were not to eat of it?"

"I can't believe I'm hearing that from you. If you thought it was such a big deal, why didn't you stop me? You were standing right there! And now you blame *me!*"

Sin corrodes all human relationships. Because each person stands like a porcupine in the center of his own world, and since he meets other porcupines guarding their turf, much can go wrong, not just in marriage, but in all human interactions. Arthur Guiterman touched on this when he said, "The porcupine, whom we must handle gloved, may be respected, but never loved!"[3] Relationships that begin with trust and care can easily deteriorate into anger, disloyalty, and finger-pointing. Secrets that were to be solemnly kept are beamed from the housetops by the person who believes that revealing them will make him/her look good.

Shame made Adam and Eve fear rejection from God and from each other. This feeling had them bound; they would spend much of their lives seeking new ways to remain hidden. Justifying their behavior to others would become an obsession. For the most part, they would retreat into denial, simply refusing to admit their personal responsibility, refusing to see themselves as others do, and even resisting what God's Word says about the human heart.

HEALTHY SHAME

Anthropologists do not often speak about guilt, but much is written about shame. The prevailing opinion is that shame comes from breaking arbitrary rules and experiencing broken relationships. It is argued that all shame is bad, since no one is really guilty of anything for which he needs forgiveness. According to this philosophy, all shame is subjective; it is a feeling that has to be unlearned.

If we take the Scriptures seriously, none of that will do. The Bible sees shame resulting from disobedience to God. Adam and Eve, as we have learned, were not ashamed before they disobeyed God, then they were ashamed. This means that there is objective shame, a valid and necessary shame because God's commandments have been broken. In

God's presence we are exposed as flawed and shameful, and deservedly so. If we do not understand this, we do not understand the gospel.

We must disagree with those psychologists who teach that the cure for all shame is to readjust how we see reality so that we no longer feel guilty. In other words, they teach that you are not wrong, but your view of the world is wrong. They have no room for objective shame, that is, shame for which we must receive God's forgiveness. Adam and Eve felt shame because they were guilty of breaking an objective standard.

Some things should shame us; we should be grateful for it. The problem with the wicked is that they have no sense of shame. "Are they ashamed of their loathsome conduct? No, they have no shame at all; they do not even know how to blush" (Jer. 6:15). We live in a culture that is shameless in the worst sense of the word. Just think of the talk shows in which every evil act is exposed to the world without a sense of shame. People think that as long as they "let it all hang out" their "honesty" will somehow relieve their guilt and resolve their conflicts. Rest assured that our society collapses when we have lost the ability to feel shame.

Jesus did not come to tell us that we should deny our feelings of shame because we are not guilty. It is precisely because we have objective shame and guilt that we need His forgiveness. Our disobedience is anarchy against God. He did not come to make us feel better (though, thanks to Him, we do), but to put our sin and shame away. We are under a curse, and it had to be removed if we were to be saved. Shame is the first step in God's gift of grace. Indeed, God puts people to shame (see Ps. 53:5). Woe to those who do not feel shame, for they cannot be redeemed.

Lewis B. Smeeds wrote, "A healthy sense of shame is perhaps the surest sign of our divine origin and our human dignity. . . . We are the closest to health when we let ourselves feel the pain of it and be led by the pain to do something about it."[4] Paul understood both the meaning of shame and the need to turn away from the practices that produce it. "Therefore, since through God's mercy we have this ministry, we do not lose heart. Rather, we have renounced secret and shameful ways; we do not use deception, nor do we distort the word of God" (2 Cor. 4:1–2).

Though shame and guilt cannot be separated, they are not identical. Even after my guilt has been removed, I can still feel shame over my past. Though we are forgiven, there are some things in our lives that, if they were known, would bring shame. In other words, shame sometimes continues after the guilt has been take away. But that sense of shame is self-generated, for God's forgiveness means that He, figuratively speaking, offers us a garment that covers our shame (see Rev. 3:18). Shame can no longer destroy us.

Millions of people live in fear today that someone is going to expose their past. They live in this tunnel of fear, hoping, praying that they will never be found out. If that should happen, they would be "ashamed." Some, in fact, actually disclose their past to a few friends, just so that if they were uncovered, they would be able to say, "Yes, what you have heard is true, but it has been dealt with." Such sharing of confidences might be a good idea.

THE SHAME-BASED HOME

If objective shame is that for which I need forgiveness, subjective shame is that which is imposed upon me by others, most likely members of my family. If healthy shame leads me to seek God's forgiveness, unhealthy shame condemns me for that which others have done, for which they should seek God's forgiveness. For example, children brought up in an alcoholic home feel shame though they have done nothing wrong. The same can be said of abused children, those who have been belittled and shamed by their parents. Recently I spoke with a rape victim who felt "dirty and ashamed" because of someone else's evil and not her own.

Such shame is a pervasive feeling that I am flawed and hopelessly defective. It is a sense of worthlessness, a feeling that there is no cure for my basic problem, for I have been permanently scarred. Shame tells me that I am condemned and abandoned to my well-deserved fate. As John Bradshaw puts it, the core of one's being can become "shame-based." He writes, "It is this dead-end quality of shame that makes it so hopeless.

The possibility of repair seems foreclosed if one is essentially flawed as a human being. Add to that the self-generating quality of shame, and one can see the devastating, soul-murdering power of neurotic shame."[5] No wonder shame lies at the core of many mental and emotional illnesses.

Let's be more specific on how such shame is communicated. Sometimes it begins with the excessive control that parents seek to have over their children. A father, for example, might unfairly and angrily overdiscipline his children. Random beatings give a child the feeling that there is nothing he can do to rectify the situation or to make himself right. If his parents are irrational, he knows he will be beaten whether he is good or bad. This feeling of powerlessness will result in intense anger and shame. As a parent he will get the opportunity to exercise the power he was denied as a child. Chances are he will treat his own children just as he himself was treated. Victims often become victimizers.

Sexual abuse also creates incredible shame. A woman who was abused said that when she went to school she thought her classmates could see inside of her; it was as if they all knew her terrible secrets. She was damaged goods and thought everyone could plainly see that it was so. She felt exposed and diminished, unable to look her teacher or friends in the eye.

Often in homes—yes, Christian homes—normal sexual curiosity is shamed. A child growing up in such an environment will feel such shame about sexual matters that years later this shame will be communicated to his children. The slightest normal sexual interest or desire is shamed by the parents in the hope that this will keep the child from sexual explorations. Of course it has the opposite effect; shame only increases curiosity, and such focused curiosity leads to a preoccupation with one's sexual desires. Thus, shame drives a child to do more shameful acts. If he is flawed anyway, what difference does it make?

A home in which there is constant ridicule, minimizing, and blaming can be considered "shame-based." Children subject to criticism or blame are shamed to the core. I've known parents brought up in shame-based homes who had an overwhelming desire to blame their children for the slightest infraction, whether real or imagined. In such an environment there is continual finger-pointing. The mother shouts, "Who put that toothbrush on the kitchen shelf? Don't you know that we don't put toothbrushes just anywhere in this house! No one in this house is going to get by with *that!*" Every incident is huge; there are no small crises.

As we have already stated, a home in which there are addictions is one with a truckload of family secrets. With this come personal isolation, emotional numbness, and distrust. The philosophy is that if you don't trust others you will never get hurt. To acknowledge a mistake is to open oneself to scrutiny. The rule is, "Cover up your own mistakes and if someone else makes a mistake, shame him."[6]

We've already learned that children need mirroring; that is, they need healthy people to reflect back to them who they really are. In the dysfunctional home, the child mirrors the parent. The parents are still children in search of someone who will be there for them. What the parent could not find in her mother, she now finds in her child. The child will always be there at her disposal, to do with as she wills. The child soon picks up on the idea that he exists to provide narcissistic gratification for the parent.[7] When a child lives with an emotionally or mentally ill parent, the child reasons, "If my parents are sick and crazy, how could I survive? It must be that I am sick or crazy."[8] Thus, the children will mirror the parent's warped view of reality.

THE EFFECTS OF UNRESOLVED SHAME

Paranoia

The effects of unresolved shame are enormous. First, there is the possibility of paranoia. The paranoid person is trying to cope with excessive shame. He is expecting betrayal and humiliation, so he interprets all events as personally threatening and lives constantly on guard. "Wrongdoings, mistakes and other instances of personal failure cannot be owned by the paranoid-type personality. They are disavowed and transferred from the inner self to others."[9]

A boy who grows up with a dominant mother who constantly belittles him and does not allow him to develop into a man grows up with shame, the conviction that he will never meet her expectations. He becomes incredibly secretive and distrustful of anyone who asks him questions or suggests improvement. He believes that others are lying in wait to expose him, to bring him to further shame and ruin. All relationships are superficial because everyone is an enemy, unless proved otherwise. He is fearful of exposure even if he is not doing anything for which he should be ashamed.

Criminal Behavior

Second, unresolved shame can lead to criminal behavior. A child growing up in an atmosphere of shame is powerless when mistreated by a parent. He has felt deep abuse and humiliation. Not knowing how to cope with the stifling effects of those who have controlled him, he lashes out in anger against his parents, against himself, and against God. Crime becomes his way of "evening the score" and finally exercising power in his powerless world.

Perfectionism

Third, those who were reared in a shame-based home can become perfectionistic.

For the perfectionist, good is never good enough. When parental love and acceptance are based only on performance, the perfectionist is created. Perfectionism "always creates a super-human measure by which one is compared."[10] Of course, this leads to angry judgmentalism, a disdain for those who don't try as hard as they should. The perfectionist cannot be vulnerable and accepting of criticism because that opens one up to the possibility of being seen as defective, which generates more shame. Perfectionism, then, is a mask to cover the shame.

Not all perfectionism is bad. When I had surgery a few months ago,

I hoped and prayed that my doctor was a perfectionist! If something is worth doing, as the saying goes, "it is worth doing right." Some things must be done just right; but there are other times when our standards are so high and our desire to blame becomes so strong that perfectionism must be seen as deadly to human relationships.

Since an entire chapter in this book is devoted to the controlling personality, I shall only make passing reference to it here. Remember, the controller is trying to make sure that he will never be shamed again. He sees himself as defective, but to make sure that no one will ever find out about this, he hides behind his perceived power, keeping everything and everyone "in line." Bradshaw writes, "For the power addict, power is the way to insulate against any further shaming. One can, through having power over others, reverse the role of early childhood."[11]

Supercriticism and blame are perhaps the most common ways that shame and inadequacy are transferred. Parents who felt put down or humiliated want to minimize the impact by putting down someone beneath them, usually their children. Those who have shame (and anger, since they often go together) find it difficult to commend others. If they do make a complimentary statement, it is usually coupled with a disclaimer. "You cleaned the kitchen, but you should have put the garbage out, too." In other words, no compliment is allowed to stand on its own. It always has to have a *but*.

A Human Doormat

Fourth, the person who feels the sting of shame often becomes a doormat for others. The person who feels flawed and defective believes that abuse is deserved; in fact, many resent expressions of genuine love and compassion. Of course, they think they are looking for someone to love them, but when an attempt is made, they react in one of two ways: Either they reject the kindness or they keep raising the bar higher, making it impossible for the person who cares about them to meet their needs.

Every weakness has its pluses, so I should mention that many who were brought up with shame become excellent and conscientious caretakers, bending over backward to help people. Caretaking plays the dual role of distracting a person from the feeling of inadequacy and providing him the affirmation of others. The negative side to this is that shame-based people often become enablers, a crutch to help an alcoholic husband or father. They feel the shame of exposure so keenly that they want to keep the addiction a secret and also receive some affirmation from someone for whom they feel a responsibility.

Obese people are often shame-bound; they feel empty, lonely, and judged. They feel that their worth is diminished because they have not met an acceptable standard of appearance that society expects. They act jovial and happy for fear of the potential shame they would experience if they expressed sorrow or anger.[12] Though being overweight might have a genetic base, for many people overeating produces a change in mood that they think they deserve. If such a person does go on a diet, it is usually "all or nothing," starving himself in the hope of having a quick fix. But because the underlying problem has not been resolved, the weight is usually put back on quickly.

If you don't think that shame is powerful, keep in mind that part of the suffering of hell is eternal shame. "Multitudes who sleep in the dust of the earth will awake: some to everlasting life, others to shame and everlasting contempt" (Dan. 12:2). Imagine being totally exposed in the sight of God, and in the presence of others, without a covering, without an opportunity to hide, without the forgiveness that only God can give. That would be hell.

GOD'S CURE FOR SHAME

We've spoken about objective shame, that is, the shame we have when we violate God's standard. We've also analyzed subjective shame, that is, the shame that has been imposed upon us by the sin of others. Either way, the healing of shame begins with the experience of grace. To quote Smeeds again, "The surest cure for the feeling of being an unacceptable person is the discovery that we are accepted by the grace of One whose acceptance matters most."[13]

When the Israelites came out of the forty years in the desert, they carried with them the stigma of shame. Shame because they refused to enter the Promised Land when they had the opportunity; shame because they had spent so much time complaining; shame because they were fearful of the future. So after they crossed the Jordan River, God took them to a place called Gilgal, which means "to roll away." We read, "Then the LORD said to Joshua, 'Today I have rolled away the reproach of Egypt from you'" (Josh. 5:9). For the past, they needed both God's forgiveness and His acceptance.

Perhaps you, dear reader, have to have the shame of your past taken away, or perhaps you know someone who does. Perhaps you were conceived out of wedlock or reared in a shame-based home. Perhaps you have done many things for which you quite rightly feel shame. To all who are afraid to crawl out from under their psychological bunkers, I have a message of hope.

Regarding those who were tempted to return to the Old Testament sacrifices as a means of salvation, the author of Hebrews says that they, in effect, recrucify Jesus and again subject Him to *"open shame"* (6:6 NASB; emphasis added). Thankfully, He was crucified but once, taking away our shame and guilt. We need not return to other sacrifices.

In an excellent article titled "Shame Crucified," Rodney Clapp discusses how Christ delivers us from shame. He says that the most dreadful thing about the Cross was not the physical suffering, but the shame. This form of execution was reserved for those least worthy of respect. The formula for sentencing to crucifixion read: "Executioner, bind his hands, veil his head, and hang him on a tree of shame."[14] It was always done publicly to emphasize its disgrace. No wonder Paul wrote, "Christ redeemed us from the curse of the law by becoming a curse for us, for it is written: 'Cursed is everyone who is hung on a tree'" (Gal. 3:13).

Let us ask a series of questions Clapp would have us answer by looking to the experience of Jesus:

Does shame bind us? Jesus was bound.

Does shame destroy our reputation? "He is despised and rejected of men."

Does shame reduce us to silence? "He is led as a lamb to the slaughter and as a sheep before his shearers is silent, so he opened not his mouth."

Does shame expose our apparent weakness? "He saved others, himself he cannot save."

Does shame lead to abandonment? "My God, my God, why have you forsaken me?"

Does shame diminish us? He was crucified naked, exposed for gawkers to see.[15]

What was Jesus' response to this shame? Again we turn to the Book of Hebrews: "Let us fix our eyes on Jesus, the author and perfecter of our faith, who for the joy set before him endured the cross, scorning its shame, and sat down at the right hand of the throne of God" (Heb. 12:2). He proved that shame cannot permanently disable; it cannot permanently cripple. Thanks to Jesus, shame has lost its power; like the sting that was removed from death, He also removed the sting of shame. To quote Clapp, "He shamed, shame."

Jesus faced shame and robbed it of its power. No kind of shame, whether objective or subjective, can ever "separate us from the love of God in Christ Jesus our Lord" (Rom. 8:39). As Clapp writes, "The Cross creates a community of people, who, no longer afraid of being defined and destroyed by shame, can admit their failures and allow their neediness."[16]

I agree with psychologist Gary Oliver, who said that people will only change when their pain is greater than their fears. Our responsibility is to create an atmosphere in which the fear is lessened, an atmoshere of honesty where love, rather than condemnation, rules. Rather than increase people's shame, we must provide a place where they can be healed without being further shamed. People try to hide their shame with denial, but it simply will not go away. Ted Roberts writes, "Therefore the church of the future, if it is to be effective, must become a place of practical grace. It must be a place where hope is the dominant theme, and denial, especially in religious pretending, is nowhere in sight."[17] The curse must be lifted.

What Needs to Be Done with Our Shame?

First, objective shame must be covered by God. When David sinned and then confessed his sin to God, he wrote, "Blessed is he whose transgressions are forgiven, whose sins are covered" (Ps. 32:1). Yes, God sewed fig leaves to cover Adam and Eve; today, we are covered by the garments of righteousness, the righteousness of Christ.

Second, our shame (whether objective or subjective) must be surrendered to God. God was with David after his hapless "cover-up" was revealed and his shameful misdeeds and crimes exposed. After his confession to God, he then knew there would be nothing revealed to those around him that was not already forgiven. If his shame in the presence of God was gone, he could now endure the ridicule of men. He would have agreed with a contemporary song that tells us, "He who knows me the best, loves me the most."

Third, we must become part of a Christian community that loves and cares about those whose lives are characterized by shame. No one is so defective but that he merits human compassion and concern. As for God, He shows His love to the vilest of sinners; those who have fallen the farthest often are blessed the most. "But where sin increased, grace increased all the more" (Rom. 5:20).

There is a pastor who committed adultery, which he confessed to a counselor. The relationship ended as quickly as it began, so he continued in the ministry for ten productive years, no one aware of his secret. Then, without provocation, the other woman decided to sue the pastor for the deed done so many years before. After the sin was exposed, the pastor resigned his position, but as he stood before the congregation he asked them this question: "Could I stay here among you and be healed by your love and acceptance?" and they said yes. So he continued to fellowship with the people he loved and received affirmation from those who loved him. He refused to let shame cut him off from the very people who could restore him back to wholeness. And without the affirmation of people, shame will retain its power.

Does the name Amnon mean anything to you? He was one of David's sons, the half brother of Absalom. Amnon fell in love with Tamar, who was his half sister. He wanted to have sexual intercourse with her, so he set a scheme into action. He pretended to be sick and requested that she come into the room to prepare some food for him. When she did this, he jumped from the bed and asked her for sex. When she said no, in anger he raped her.

After the ordeal, we read, "Amnon hated her with a very great hatred; for the hatred with which he hated her was greater than the love with which he had loved her. And Amnon said to her, 'Get up, go away!'" (2 Sam. 13:15 NASB). We can only imagine the shame Tamar felt. She had resisted him, and now that he had defiled her he treated her like dirt. She had done nothing to make him angry; yet look at his anger!

He asked her to leave his presence, but she refused, arguing that sending her away would compound the evil. Amnon would hear none of it and asked his attendant to throw the woman out and lock the door.

She was destroyed by shame.

Let us hear her cries: "And Tamar put ashes on her head, and tore her long-sleeved garment which was on her [a symbol of her virginity]; and she put her hand on her head and went away, crying aloud as she went" (2 Sam. 13:19 NASB). The ashes symbolized her shame and humiliation.

Freedom from Shame

What does God do for people like this? How can those who are overcome by shame be free, no longer captive to those who have tried to demean and destroy them? Three blessings are given to the nation Israel, shamed by defeat. "Instead of their shame my people will receive a double portion, and instead of disgrace they will rejoice in their inheritance . . . and everlasting joy will be theirs" (Isa. 61:7).

The specifics are spelled out a few verses before the one just quoted. Isaiah predicts that with the coming of Christ, the brokenhearted will receive healing and those in prison will be released. Those who mourn will be comforted. And He will "bestow on them a crown of beauty instead of ashes, the oil of gladness instead of mourning, and a garment of praise instead of a spirit of despair" (v. 3).

First, he gives them a crown of beauty instead of ashes. He removes the ashes of humiliation and replaces them with a garland, which is an ornamental headdress used for times of rejoicing. Yes, this turban was worn for festive occasions and was a symbol of prosperity and victory. God takes the shame away and gives the gift of beauty.

Second, He gives them "the oil of gladness instead of mourning." Perfumed ointment was poured on guests at joyous feasts. David wrote of the special treatment God gives to those He loves: "He anoints my head with oil, my cup runs over." It was a high honor to be anointed with soothing oil, a symbol of the grace God gives to those who have been abused, mourning for their sin and those of others. The funeral will give way to the wedding.

Third, He will give them "a garment of praise instead of a spirit of despair." The stigma of their shame will be covered. Their clothing will be bright and beautiful, not drab and "make do." When God gives us clothing it is not only bright, but clean.

These three blessings are promised to the Israelites shamed by defeat. These outward symbols will be a sign of inner healing. The new look without is to remind them of the new joy within. The conclusion is, "They will be called oaks of righteousness, a planting of the LORD, for the display of his splendor" (Ps. 61:3).

A minister who committed immorality and had to resign in disgrace told me, "Just think of peeling an onion, and as you do, layer after layer comes off, but there is nothing in the center. There was nothing left, just myself and God. Because of shame I retreated from every friend who ever knew me. I was despised, spoken about—and I deserved whatever was said about me. I wondered how I could get up in the morning and put one foot ahead of another."

As we drove together in his car, he put a cassette in the stereo.

> Calvary covers it all
> My past with its sin and stain [read shame]
> My guilt and despair
> Jesus took on Him there
> And Calvary covers it all.

You say, "But nothing will ever be the same for him again." That is true, it won't. In the end his sin destroyed his marriage and impacted his children. Neither was it the same for Adam and Eve. But God gave them garments to wear, and He does the same for us. All that we can do is give Him the broken pieces and trust Him to heal our souls.

Remember, the purpose of the Cross was to repair the irreparable; it is God's answer to the fragments of our lives that can never be put back together. That's why we read that those who put their trust in God will never be put to shame—they can never be finally and wholly destroyed.

Let's take the advice of the Wonderful Counselor: "I counsel you to buy from me gold refined in the fire, so you can become rich; and white clothes to wear, *so you can cover your shameful nakedness;* and salve to put on your eyes, so you can see" (Rev. 3:18; emphasis added). God has made provision for our human condition. There is more grace in His heart than there is shame in our past.

A Promise to Ponder

Do not be afraid; you will not suffer shame.
Do not fear disgrace; you will not be humiliated.
You will forget the shame of your youth and remember
no more the reproach of your widowhood.

—Isa. 54:4

CHAPTER 6
THE ROOTS OF RAGE

Bobby knight, newly appointed head basketball coach at Texas Tech University, was fired from his previous position at Indiana University for what can best be called "a temper problem." He was in the habit of working himself into what one writer called "a competitive lather" and was unable to restrain his outbursts. Since he was often out of control, he found himself out of a job for a period of time.

Anger is one of the most common emotions. If you have lived, you have been angry. Perhaps extremely angry. Medical doctors Walter Byrd and Paul Warren believe that "anger is one of the first and foremost means for honest interaction with one's environment."[1] Children use anger as a coping device to adapt to difficult situations. We've all known toddlers whose temper tantrums reflected frustration because of desires that were denied. This is a natural, if not a healthy, response when circumstances do not line up with one's plans and wishes. Children, of course, must be taught to control their anger in healthy ways. If anger is out of control, it is often called rage, that powerful force that destroys, ruins, and terrifies.

In marriage counseling it is almost impossible for two angry partners to see one another objectively; every perception is skewed by anger. One of the best assignments you can give an angry couple is this: Put yourself in the shoes of your partner and write a letter from your mate to yourself saying what he or she would say given the opportunity to speak. She writes a letter he would write; he writes a letter she would write. This will force the partners to look at the relationship through their mate's set of glasses. This is an important step toward objectivity.

Anger is not always sin. "'In your anger do not sin': Do not let the sun go down while you are still angry," Paul wrote (Eph. 4:26). We should be angry with injustice, with evil, and with the stubbornness of the human heart. Of Jesus we read, "He looked around at them in anger and, deeply distressed at their stubborn hearts, said . . ." (Mark 3:5).

Anger is often the basis of motivation; those who are angry at the right things can move mountains to see their vision accomplished. Wilberforce was angry at slavery, Luther was angry with the indulgence traffic, and Martin Luther King was angry about racism. Each of these people, and others like them, sparked a reformation; they changed the moral and spiritual landscape of their times because they became angry with abuses. Yes, it is possible to be "good and angry."

But anger distorts perception. Two men had an argument, and in a fit of rage, one killed the other. The murderer felt deep regret for the death of a man he had once considered a friend, but the deed could not be undone. Imagine waking up every day in prison for the next thirty years, going through the routine of prison life, flooded with regret and shame over one's actions. Anger can make us do in a moment what cannot be recovered in a lifetime.

Most anger is masked; it is skillfully hidden beneath the surface of one's psyche. Ask the parents of the Columbine gunmen if they suspected that their children were angry and violent and they will tell you that no, they did not think their sons were capable of such crimes. When Mark Barton killed his wife, children, and nine others, a neighbor said that he had been a good role model and added, "It makes you feel as if you don't know anyone."[2]

I've met people who were calm and collected, but I discovered later that they had a burning cauldron of anger deep within. Many a distraught wife has said after marriage, "I didn't know that he could get violent; he rages out of control. I wonder what it will be like if we have children." Such rage follows no pattern; a man might be angry one day for something he will overlook the next day.

DOMESTIC VIOLENCE

Former United States surgeon general C. Everett Koop labels domestic abuse "the number one health problem in America."[3] Back in the early 1990s, *Time* reported that one-third of all women who arrive at a doctor's office or hospital seeking emergency treatment are victims of domestic violence.[4] As more and more of our children are reared in broken homes and are sexually abused, the victims take their anger into their own marriages; thus, battered wives are legion.

It is almost impossible to give a profile of an abuser. Many abusers are charming and well liked. They are well dressed, have a social conscience, and enjoy an impeccable reputation. One day they adore their wives, and the next they beat them. Because their abusive personality is so well hidden, even their close friends have no idea that they are socializing with an abuser. This explains why many unsuspecting women do not know they've married an abuser until after the wedding. Now that the relationship is secure and the wife has no easy way out, the abuse can begin.

Abuse takes many forms. There is physical abuse: slapping, hitting, choking, or the like. But if an abuser thinks he might get into trouble with the law, he will resort to verbal and emotional abuse. In this way he can destroy his wife while insisting he isn't hurting anyone. So he uses curses, threats, belittling, and economic punishment (the wife has to beg for every dime she gets and give a personal account for every dime she spends). Or he will resort to emotional abuse, blaming his wife for everything he has done. He will say, "You made me hit you." Or, "It is your fault that I lost my temper."

Abusers are very strict in their expectations; they gravitate to the letter of the law, often using the Bible as their authority. They will find a technical reason why they have a right to get angry, and it will always be the spouse's fault. Remember, at this point the abuser might be incapable of taking responsibility for his actions. Needless to say, God holds him accountable, and so should we.

Don't lose sight of the abuser's goal: He uses anger to "destabilize" his wife so that she will not only keep his behavior a secret but will believe that it is all her fault. His accusations and threats so distort her perceptions that she actually ends up believing that she is responsible for his actions. He wants her to feel utterly helpless, that she lacks the power to change the situation. He has made her believe that if she goes for help no one will believe her anyway, since he is highly respected at work, in his neighborhood, and at church. He will resort to physical violence if he thinks he is losing control.

Such abusers have deep hidden resentments and are angry almost all the time. Because this resentment is unconscious, it is often denied. Such a person becomes defensive and angry when told that he is angry. The man who jabs his fist in the air, with his neck and face becoming crimson, shouting, "I'm not angry!" is not a joke. Some of you reading these pages know such an individual. If he admits that he is angry, he blames others for it.

The actions of the abuser are unpredictable. He might come home in a good mood, but the slightest matter might send him into a rage. No one knows what spark will ignite the gasoline. This unpredictability makes those around him "walk on eggshells." As a result, meaningful communication is, of course, stifled. Quietness, when it comes, is so welcome that the wife and children will want to "lie low" to minimize the possibility of an eruption of rage.

The children might not be directly abused, but they are often used as weapons of control and anger. The more the mother loves the child, the more the father will do what he can to isolate the child from her mother. A father who shows no special love for the child might fight for custody in the divorce battle, not only so he can deceive himself into believing that he is a caring father, but also to vent anger toward his wife.

Should such a man ask for forgiveness—and some abusers do—the wife is pleased, thinking that the man has turned over a new leaf. But alas, he repeats his behavior, because the roots of rage are deep. A promise of reform from a hot-tempered man should be accepted with the same skepticism as one accepts a promise of sobriety from an alcoholic. Yes, there might be repentance, but it is too shallow, too little understood. Most angry people have no idea of the depth of their problem.

Someone has said that marriage is the "mad factory." Because it is the most intimate of all relationships, it is here that resentments are stored for later use. Two selfish people coming together in marriage are bound to have conflicts, but when one of the partners is seething with rage, the conflicts escalate. Rage is the tree; resentment and bitterness are the roots beneath the ground.

Let's not think that only men struggle with rage; women can do so as well. They might deal with it differently (as we shall see in a moment), but the effects in a marriage are essentially the same. But I have a word especially to the women reading these pages: If you are married to an abuser, defy his threats and get help! No matter how many promises he makes, he probably will not change until he acknowledges his need and has counsel and accountability. Your willingness to put up with the situation is only a further stimulus for him to maintain the fiction of innocence.

Why do good people do bad things? Their anger brings misery to those around them and sends their own lives spiraling out of control, smashing relationships that can never be repaired.

KINDS OF ANGER

There are three different kinds of anger mentioned in the Bible and confirmed by observation and experience. The first two words we will consider are found in Ephesians: "Get rid of all bitterness, rage [thumos] and anger [orge], brawling and slander, along with every form of malice. Be kind and compassionate to one another, forgiving each other, just as in Christ God forgave you" (4:31–32). The first word is thumos, which means "a turbulent commotion, an explosion of temper or rage." This is the pit bull kind of anger; it is the rage that destroys, the rage that abuses.

A second word is *orge,* which means "a long-lasting attitude that continues to seek revenge"; it could also be defined as "resentment." This kind of anger reminds us of the cobra, which carries out its schemes with cunning, methodical, devious, emotionless planning. This kind of anger can abuse, deceive, and blame without a twinge of conscience. What distinguishes it from *thumos* (the pit bull anger) is that *orge* is usually not out of control. In fact, the person with this kind of anger takes pride in his ability to remain calm and collected as his schemes are carried out. He is the kind of person who will clean his gun in the presence of his wife, just to remind her of what could happen were she to defy him.

The third Greek word for anger is *aganaktesis,* which means "indignation"; it is the kind of indignation that usually brings about appropriate behavior. Of course, there is not a neat division between these kinds of anger in real life. Some abusers might act like a pit bull one day, a cobra the next, and be appropriately indignant the day after that. In any case, the person who is filled with rage might be charming, intimidating, and cunning. Interestingly, in the Old Testament Hebrew, the word most often translated *anger* is *aph,* which means "nostrils." This is a word picture of someone whose nostrils are flared or snorting with anger. We sometimes speak of someone who is "hot under the collar," that is, someone whose blood vessels are inflamed because of anger.

THE CAUSES OF RAGE

What are the roots of rage? How does the pit bull or the cobra develop? We will discover the answer in the first story of rage found in the Bible.

> Abel kept flocks, and Cain worked the soil. In the course of time
> Cain brought some of the fruits of the soil as an offering to the
> LORD. But Abel brought fat portions from some of the firstborn of
> his flock. The LORD looked with favor on Abel and his offering, but
> on Cain and his offering he did not look with favor. So Cain was
> very angry, and his face was downcast.

Then the LORD said to Cain, "Why are you angry? Why is your face downcast? If you do what is right, will you not be accepted? But if you do not do what is right, sin is crouching at your door; it desires to have you, but you must master it."

Now Cain said to his brother Abel, "Let's go out to the field." And while they were in the field, Cain attacked his brother Abel and killed him. (Gen. 4:2–8)

What drove Cain to kill his brother? Rejection, belittling, and power-lessness.

Abusive Parents

Cain was rejected by God, and his brother was accepted. Look into the lives of those who struggle with rage and you will often find jealousy and rejection. This explains why abusive parents produce angry children. The children are angry because they feel that they have been unfairly treated. People who feel cheated often have an overwhelming sense of anger toward those who have "done them in." They seethe with resentment and want to "show them a thing or two."

Children can become angry quickly, but they are also quick to forgive. In their early years they do not carry resentments. That is why Paul says, "In regard to evil be infants" (1 Cor. 14:20). But as they grow older, their anger might turn into hostility. If they were reared in a home in which they were unfairly treated, if they feel the sting of rejection, if they were not allowed to express their anger, they will shut down emotionally. But beneath the surface lies the cauldron of anger.

The best homes are those in which children are told that it is okay to be angry but they must control their responses. Then through dialogue and understanding they might feel that they can resolve it and leave it behind. If anger is not dealt with in a healthy way, it becomes resentment.

Cain felt anger for a related reason: He felt belittled and diminished. His brother had received God's blessing, but he had been left out, relegated to second best. We've all been angry when a motorist has cut into the lane ahead of us. We might get to our destination thirty seconds later, a small amount of time to be sure. What makes us angry is not that we arrive later. Rather, it is the feeling that the rude motorist has belittled us, that he has made us feel that his agenda is more important than ours. We wish we could teach him a lesson about our own importance. In Chicago a man pulled a gun and shot at the man who switched into his lane, in the process wounding a toddler who will have brain damage for the rest of her life. That is "road rage."

During the days of the gasoline crunch, one driver shot another at a gas station because the man had cut into the line ahead of him. The wronged driver flew into a rage. "So you think that I am less than you, that my schedule isn't as important than yours? I'll show you who is boss around here!" And the gun went off. Check the background of those students responsible for the recent high-school shootings and you will find deep anger because they felt ignored or diminished.

Improper Sexual Relationships

Improper sexual relationships are the cause of much anger. A young woman gives herself to her boyfriend, based on a promise of love or marriage. Having satisfied his desires, he is with another woman by the next week. The young woman feels slighted, taken for granted, humiliated, betrayed, shamed, and abused. Her resentment will be carried into the next relationship and, if not properly processed, will affect her future marriage and all of her friendships.

Powerlessness

Another related root of rage is powerlessness. When you feel that you have been unfairly treated and that nothing can be done about it, you might hold your anger for a time, but when the time is right, you will want to lash out. We've spoken about the child in an abusive home who knows that no matter how he acts, he will be beaten anyway. He submits to it, for his father is stronger than he is, but the anger builds. When he is married he will at last be able to "show who is boss" and take out his anger on his wife and children.

Strictly speaking, Cain was not powerless, since he could have taken God's advice and also been accepted. But in the stubbornness of his heart, he chose to defy God, insisting that if the offering he brought was not satisfactory, so be it. Those who feel marginalized, wounded, and unable to change their situations often develop deep-seated anger. Injustice, without a remedy, leads many to frustration and irrational revenge.

Shame

Shame is also a cause of anger. As we learned in the previous chapter, if you grew up in a shame-based home you might struggle with anger. Anger because of how you were treated, anger because you fear to be shamed again, anger because no one seems to meet your expectations. Take that into your marriage, and you will soon discover conflict with your spouse and recycled anger in the lives of your children.

THE CONSEQUENCES OF UNRESOLVED ANGER

You've heard it said, "I just blow up and let it all hang out, but when it's over, it's over." Yes, for the person who has just blown up it might be over, but it is not over for those who received the brunt of the anger; for them it is never over. This is why we read in Proverbs, "Better a patient man than a warrior, a man who controls his temper [is better] than one who takes a city" (16:32).

Years ago therapists believed that anger had to "come out." So they thought of "appropriate" ways to release the anger. The counselee was given a pillow and was asked to pretend that it was the person with whom he was angry, perhaps his mother-in-law. He was told he could "attack it for all he was worth." But such "venting" only inflamed the anger. Once again we are reminded that a superficial diagnosis of our problem leads to a superficial cure.

If it is wrong to "blow up," it is also wrong to "clam up." We've spoken about anger that turns into resentment, a kind of anger that turns into passivity and aggression. This is expressed through procrastination, stubbornness, and intentional inefficiency. The person is saying, "I'll do all that I can to obstruct you because of how I feel about you."

A passive-aggressive person will always try to make things difficult at meetings, always making short meetings long by trying to impede progress. He wants to know who has taken what side of the dispute so that he can oppose others with more confidence. In effect, his motto is, "If you are for it, I'm against it." Of course, his anger is skillfully hidden, but at root, he is taking out his anger on all those around him.

The passive-aggressive wife might deliberately take more time getting ready for church than is strictly necessary. This is true especially if she knows that her husband is compulsive about being on time. She will methodically go about the kitchen and the bedroom, taking her sweet time in getting ready; she will show no visible hint of anger, but she knows exactly what she is doing. She is saying to herself, *I'll just let him wait.*

Once in the car, she will say nothing. But of course her husband is furious, so he begins to berate her for being late. She calmly replies, "Well, I have more to do in the morning than you. . . . I didn't see you helping me prepare breakfast or make the bed." She knows she has him exactly where she wants him: angry, without an argument that she cannot answer. As they pull up to the church, she gives her parting shot as she calmly says, "I hope you have a good day teaching your Sunday school class. . . . Is the topic anger?" Of course she won't admit to anger, because she is calm and controlled. The arrow of her resentment has hit its mark, though she did not raise her voice or say one unplanned word.

The passive-aggressive person might use humor to mask his anger. He might tease a child, and when the child cries, he will say, "I was just joking." But the real reason for the "fun" is to humiliate the child, to bring him to a point of anger and despair. The angry parent whose discipline is often overbearing and erratic communicates anger to the child. When the child becomes a teenager, he might dress in a way that displeases his parents. If his parents detest purple, the son might have his hair dyed purple and, for the first time, sit in the front row in church. If his parents dislike the girl he is dating, he will marry her to irritate them. He might spend the rest of his life reacting to the kind of person they wanted him to be. In his heart it's payback time.

A woman who has been abused by men will carry that anger into her marriage unless the root of the resentment is identified and dealt with. Like all of us, she must forgive those who have taken advantage of her, or her anger and distrust will be passed on to those around her. Because of her insecurities and perfectionism, the temptation will be to be supercritical, negative, and suspicious. If her husband so much as notices another woman, she will begin to make accusations, assuming the worst.

An angry woman will make her husband jump through all kinds of hoops, and should he succeed in meeting her expectations, she will change the rules so that he will fail again. One passive-aggressive woman angrily threw the flowers her husband brought her to the floor because they were not properly cut; the next time he brought her uncut flowers, but that was not what she wanted. Something was always wrong with the flowers. On and on the cycle went, as a protective shell was developed to make sure that her husband would never please her but would of necessity be in the wrong all the time.

We've already emphasized what happens if a man does not forgive those who have wronged him. He might become a driven person, always trying to succeed, but never accomplishing success. There will be a hand on his shoulder driving him to bigger and better things; and even when he accomplishes his goals, the bar will be put up a notch. His perfectionism will not only drive him and his family, but it will also exasperate those who have to work with him. Good will never be good enough.

Of course, all of his anger will be masked. He will argue that if a job is worth doing, it is worth doing right, and there is some truth to that statement. He will insist that the Bible tells us we should be successful. If he is not picking up dishes from the cupboard and throwing them against the wall, he will tell himself that his problem isn't anger, it's just the incompetence and thoughtlessness of the people around him. No wonder one missionary leader said that the greatest problem with interpersonal relationships on the mission field is perfectionism. Perfectionists expect everyone to fold towels the way they do, discipline their children the way they do, and minister the way they do. Remember, for a perfectionist the proper standard of conduct is themselves, and they don't even meet their own goals.

CONFRONTING THE ROOTS OF RAGE

Does God deliver people from burning rage? In his book *Angry Men and the Women Who Love Them,* Paul Hegstrom tells the story of his own marriage to Judy. Six months after he accepted Christ as Savior at the age of nine, he was sexually molested by a man in the neighborhood. Paul felt dirty and damaged, but he could not talk to his parents about such matters because anything that had to do with sex was taboo.

In desperation, the boy asked his mother this hypothetical question: "If David down the street was molested by someone, what would happen to him?" To which his mother replied, "You could never play with him because he would be a marked child. He would be ruined and damaged by the things, and he would know things children should not know about."[6] Imagine what effect her answer had on this nine-year-old boy! She did not know she had condemned her own son to a life of shame and silence! Since he was not allowed to deal with the truth, that incident was held in his subconscious mind for the next thirty years.

By the time he married, he had developed a Jekyll-and-Hyde personality. He could be charming and funny, but also abusive and angry. Like most angry men, he thought he had to possess a woman, so he and Judy married young. On the first day of their honeymoon, he began to abuse her. Specifically, he got into an argument with her brother and when Judy wanted them to calm down he shoved her out of the room, causing her to fall, and yelled, "This is none of your business."

Like many abusers, he asked forgiveness but reminded her that this was really her fault, because she had tried to intervene in the argument. So, on that first day of their honeymoon, Judy learned to take the blame for his violent outbursts. What followed were years of increasingly unpredictable abuse. Paul was in denial, blaming her for everything. Eventually they separated for three and a half years and then were divorced for three and a half. But, thanks be to God, fifteen years ago they remarried and so far have not had one instance of physical or emotional abuse.

How did God deliver Paul from being an abuser? For one thing, Paul was willing to go for counseling to surface the anger that lay deeply embedded in his subconscious. He had to resurrect the anger that he had toward his abuser so that he could choose to forgive those who had wronged him. All of this did not happen at once, for he had to break through the layers of denial and a basic unwillingness to face the truth. But face it he did. Without both honesty and forgiveness, there can be no freedom from fits of rage.

Abusers must come to the realization that no series of steps for overcoming abuse will help unless they are applied. They also should know that these steps are not necessarily in sequence, and they have to be repeated many times. And yes, admitting to what has been so long denied is painful.

Admit to Anger

First, *you must admit that you are angry.* Some find this easy, since, for them, it is quite obvious. Some, quite honestly, are not aware of the anger that lies beneath the surface, undetected after years of emotional numbness and denial. Anger, as we are learning, is like an iceberg; most of it lies beneath the conscious mind. For some, admitting their anger would expose a part of themselves that they had hoped they would never have to face. Only God can take His telescope and give us a picture of our hearts, a picture that we might not be able to handle all at once. But if we wait in silence in God's presence, He will show us what we need to know.

This admission of our need must be shared with those who are a part of the believing community. Nothing bonds people together like the acknowledgment of weaknesses and the communication of a sincere heart. Let us never forget that the church is the body of Christ; and this body, like a human body, has within itself the strength to give healing to every part. The acceptance and understanding of other believers are always essential to rehabilitation and the strengthening of the "inner man."

God's Counsel

Second, as a believer, *we must realize that Jesus was rejected to secure our acceptance.*

How would you like to be counseled by God? People often seek out pastors and counselors to solicit their advice and help them with their problems. But imagine having the privilege of receiving instructions directly from the Lord Himself! Surely we would obey the Lord, if only He spoke to us! Incredibly, Cain did not. He heard the voice of the only One who could have helped him receive the acceptance he craved, but he turned the other way.

"Then the LORD said to Cain, 'Why are you angry? Why is your face downcast? If you do what is right, will you not be accepted? But if you do not do what is right, sin is crouching at your door; it desires to have you, but you must master it'" (Gen. 4:6–7). Cain could have changed his ways; he could have been just as acceptable as his brother. But he would have none of it. The very next verse tells us that he lured his brother into the field and, in a fit of rage, killed him.

From my heart to yours: If you have been rejected in life; if you are angry because of abuse or lost opportunities or because you have been diminished by others, you can be as acceptable to God as any of the saints who have ever lived. For we all must be received by God on the same basis: We are declared as righteous as Christ Himself through faith in Him. The message of the Cross is that Christ got our sin and we get His righteousness.

Virtually all angry people were brought up in a home that was "performance-based," that is, where approval (if it was given at all) was only given when a task was done according to expectations. Now, as a child of God, you can rejoice in the sure knowledge of God's unconditional love for those who believe in His Son. Jesus was willing to be forsaken by the Father on the Cross so that we would never be forsaken by Him.

Forgiveness

Third, *we must forgive those who have wronged us.* Immediately after the exhortation for us to lay aside anger, Paul writes, "Be kind and compassionate to one another, forgiving each other, just as in Christ God forgave you" (Eph. 4:32). You must forgive those who have abused you, humiliated you, and belittled you. You must forgive those who took advantage of your weakness. Have not these individuals already robbed you of your happiness? Must they continue to control you, demanding your attention and psychic energy?

> The man I hate may be many miles from my bedroom; but more
> cruel than any slave driver, he whips my thoughts into such a frenzy
> that my innerspring mattress becomes a rack of torture. The lowliest
> of serfs can sleep, but not I. I really must acknowledge the fact that I
> am a slave to every man on whom I pour the vials of my wrath.[7]

Forgiveness differs from reconciliation. You can forgive those who wrong you without their cooperation. Forgiveness is both an act and a process. It is a choice you make and a choice you keep making every day of your life. Many people think that they have forgiven, but they have not. They might not feel any rage toward those who have wronged them, but the resentment is still there. We must continually be submitting these feelings to God.

You must also "forgive God"; that is, you must release any bitterness you have in your heart toward Him. Of course, strictly speaking, God does not need to be forgiven. But the fact is that many people are deeply angry that God has brought circumstances into their lives that could have been avoided. God stands behind everything that happens in His world. He does not do evil, but that evil is a part of His plan cannot be denied.

You must be willing to surrender the control of your life and your circumstances to God. "See to it that no one misses the grace of God and that no bitter root grows up to cause trouble and defile many" (Heb. 12:15). We must see the effects of our bitterness.

Resist Satan's Lies

Fourth, *we must realize that Satan is actively involved in the lives of those who are uncontrollably angry.* The New Testament gives this commentary on Cain: "Do not be like Cain, who belonged to the evil one and murdered his brother" (1 John 3:12). Satan uses anger to gain a foothold in the lives of those who would destroy others through words and deeds (see Eph. 4:26–27). He must be firmly resisted through the power of the Scriptures and submission to God. This can be done through the proper use of Scripture, and private and corporate prayer.

Accountability

Fifth, *there must be accountability and a commitment to put distance between yourself and the provocative situations that erupt in anger.* Since the Lord is slow to anger, we should be, too. "My dear brothers, take note of this: Everyone should be quick to listen, slow to speak and slow to become angry, for man's anger does not bring about the righteous life that God desires" (James 1:19–20). If we ask God to set a watch before our mouths, we will develop sensitivity to the Holy Spirit, whose fruit in our lives brings self-control.

Someone shared this story with me:

In a seminary classroom, a professor, whom we will call Brother Smith, was known for his elaborate object lessons. This day was no exception. On the wall he placed a big target, and on a nearby table were many darts. Brother Smith told the students to draw a picture of someone they disliked or someone they actually hated. Then he would allow them to throw darts at the person's picture.

One lady drew a picture of a girl who had stolen her boyfriend; another drew a picture of a man who had mistreated her. All of the students found someone they hated, and did so very quickly; for some the challenge was to choose just one among many.

The class lined up and began throwing darts, with much laughter and hilarity. Some of the students threw their darts with such force that their targets were ripping apart.

Just then, Brother Smith interrupted the students and removed the target from the wall. Underneath the target was a picture of Jesus.

A hush fell over the room as each student viewed the mangled picture of Jesus; holes and jagged marks covered His face, and His eyes were pierced out. Brother Smith said simply, "Inasmuch as you have done it to the least of these My brethren, you have done it unto Me."

No other words were necessary as tears filled the eyes of the students; they could not take their eyes off the picture of Jesus. Even after the bell they sat in their seats, until one slowly left and then another. Every dart you throw at your wife, your husband, or a friend lands in the heart of Jesus.

We will never deal with the roots of rage unless we know the meaning of forgiveness; we will never deal with these roots until we know the meaning of acceptance. And we will never be free until we know the wonder of Jesus.

A Promise to Ponder

Bear with each other and forgive whatever grievances

you may have against one another.

Forgive as the Lord forgave you.

And over all these virtues put on love,

which binds them all together in perfect unity.

—COL. 3:13–14

CHAPTER 7
LISTENING FOR YOUR FATHER'S VOICE

I LIVE IN A VACUUM that is as lonely as a radio tube when the batteries are dead and there is no current to plug into." Those are the words of Ernest Hemingway, who one Sunday morning in Idaho blew his head off with a shotgun blast back in 1961.

Hemingway was a man who was married four times, was in love with booze, and traveled the world without conscience or moral code. Yet he grew up in Oak Park, Illinois, steeped in the roots of evangelical Christianity. How did the life of a boy who grew up in a Christian home end so tragically? So dreadfully?

His grandparents on his father's side studied at Wheaton College during the 1860s; by all accounts they were brilliant, committed Christians. Grandfather Anson had been honorably discharged from the 72nd Infantry during the Civil War, and Grandmother Adelaide, who studied botany and chemistry, gave the valedictory address at her graduation and taught school on the side. She had a great love for nature, which was communicated to Ernest's father and then eventually to the boy himself.[1]

Anson, who became the general secretary of the YMCA, met D. L. Moody and had a close friendship with him until Moody's death in 1899 (which was the same year his famous grandson, Ernest, was born). The couple moved to Oak Park, a suburb of Chicago, where they had six children, all of whom attended Oberlin College, a fine Christian school at that time. One son served as a missionary physician in China; another son, Ed, became a physician in Oak Park and was the father of Ernest.

Hemingway's grandfather on his mother's side of the family was even more respected for his spiritual leadership. Indeed, his grandchildren called him "Abba," as if God Himself were looking at them through his eyes. He led prayers at Grace Episcopal Church in Oak Park with the grandchildren watching and participating. After the death of his wife, he moved in with the Hemingways, leading in prayer and devotions and warning against sin. As for Ernest's parents, they followed in the godly lifestyle of the grandparents. Little Ernest was baptized at Oak Park's First Congregational Church. As he grew up, his mother encouraged him to love nature and, more important, to love the God of nature, as much as she did.

His father, Ed the physician, was intelligent but rigid in his faith and discipline. Even when the children were sitting on his lap, if he recalled something they had done or said that he deemed improper or a duty they had neglected, he would order the children to their rooms without supper. The children were spanked hard across his knee, and when it was over they were ordered to pray and ask God's forgiveness. Ed was a Sunday school teacher, at war with sin. One day he drove the children to the state prison in Joliet, Illinois, so that they could see the iron bars, the stone walls, and the barbed-wire fences. He warned that this was where they would end if they did not follow the Lord and stay clear of the sins of the world.

As for little Ernest, one biographer writes, "Sin scared the life out of Ernest. At night he prayed that he had been a good boy during the day. The trouble was, a boy could never be sure that he had been good; he might have done something bad and not known it was bad. It was so hard to obey every rule, so hard to please his mother, his father, his teachers, his minister, his God; so hard that sometimes it wasn't worth trying, and the boy felt like giving up."[2]

Yet, Ernest loved his father and his father loved him. His mother, however, in love with nature, was flighty; she did not want to take care of the dirty clothes, the diapers, and the meals. She had sacrificed her career in opera to marry Ed, and she felt that this gave her the right to have her demands met. Ernest resented his mother because his father had to do double duty as both cook and breadwinner. For her part, she "waltzed about the house in long dresses, performing her music for anyone who would listen."[3]

Ernest was a good Sunday school pupil who read every word of the King James Version of the Bible to win a contest. As he grew older, he became the program chairman of the church and the treasurer and gave speeches on behalf of the church. This is the young man who would eventually find his life as empty as a disconnected radio tube and who would condemn his Christian upbringing with every ounce of his being.

After his stint as an ambulance driver in World War I, Ernest went to northern Michigan and began writing his short stories. Since he could not get them published, his parents heaped condemnation on him for not getting a steady job. Even as they prayed for him, he was writing more stories that reflected bitter disillusionment about life, the family, and Christianity. Though his father was more charitable, his mother said that he was no longer welcome in her presence.

Ernest married and sailed to Paris, where he published his first book, the content of which shocked his parents. And after his marriage broke up, the breach with his family was, for all intents and purposes, complete. They believed that he had disgraced them, the church in Oak Park, and God. In effect, he was disowned.

Dr. Hemingway became ill with diabetes and was deeply depressed. In his despondency he shot himself in his upstairs bedroom using the pistol his father—the Wheaton College alumnus—had passed down to him. Ernest was crushed, and he blamed his mother, believing she had pushed his father over the brink. In his heart, he also knew that he was at fault for having betrayed his family and his Christian roots.

Ernest's grief and guilt caused him to spiral out of control. He began a relentless attack against Oak Park, its values, its families, and its churches. He married three more times, and he spent much of his life drunk. A friend said of him, "He lived inside bad dreams." He hated his mother, and when she sent him a birthday cake along with the pistol his father had used to kill himself, Ernest got the message that she was urging him to do the same. He fulfilled his mother's perceived wish on that fateful day in 1961.

Something went terribly wrong between the day he was baptized in the Oak Park First Congregational Church and the day he died sixty-two years later. On the day of his baptism his mother wrote that she dedicated him "as an offering unto the Lord to receive His name and henceforth to be counted as one of God's little lambs." I do not absolve Ernest, since he will have to give an account to God for the life he lived. But we would be blind not to see a connection between the rejection he experienced from his parents and the lifestyle he chose to live.

THE POWER OF PARENTS

There are some lessons here for us. First of all, when the standards in a home are unrealistic and too rigid, children rebel, knowing that they can't live up to their parents' expectations anyway. If they are going to be berated for falling short, it might as well be for something decadent they chose to do. Ernest's parents are to be commended for teaching him the Bible, but they are to be faulted for demanding strict and uncompromising obedience to their faith and moral code. There is a fine line between bringing children up "in the nurture and admonition of the Lord," which is a command of Scripture (Eph. 6:4 KJV), and a failure to trust the Holy Spirit to bring about an obedience from the inside out.

I believe that Henry Blackaby is right when he says that parents who try to rigidly control their children (particularly when they become adults) actually hinder the power of God in their children's lives. There comes a time when parents must commit their children to the Lord and no longer chide them for their lifestyles. They must love their children with patient love.

When will we learn that our warnings against sin will never motivate a child to holiness unless those warnings are combined with huge doses of unconditional love. Those who have motivated me most to pursue God are not the Pharisees who saw it as their duty to demand conformity to their rules, but those whose lives proved that a close walk with God was not only possible but eminently satisfying.

When children are brought up in a home in which achievements are ignored (often because of the false notion that the children will become prideful) and in which failures are severely dealt with, they grow up with both insecurities and anger. One such child said he will never become a Christian as long as his father is alive, because he would not want to give his father the satisfaction of knowing that his son was "in the fold." Resentment has deep roots.

Second, children rejected by their parents often reject everything their parents represent. When a child does not have the unconditional love of his parents, he finds it difficult to maintain his emotional and spiritual equilibrium. Of course, the Hemingways could not approve of their son's lifestyle, but it was wrong to tell him he was no longer welcome in their presence.

There is a third lesson: Our first understanding of God is derived from how we view our parents, particularly our father. Hemingway assumed that if he was rejected by his Christian father, he was rejected by God. But, as we know, if he had sought God he could have received forgiveness and acceptance, whether his parents welcomed him or not. But in the mind of a child, the voice of the parents is, in effect, the voice of God. This is particularly true in a Christian home, in which the parents are the interpreters of God's will.

Our parents, particularly our fathers, exert powerful and lasting impact upon us for good or ill, for better or worse. When Ernest's father shot himself and then his mother sent Ernest the gun along with his birthday cake, Ernest felt he had to follow in his father's footsteps. The last prophecy of the Old Testament says that Elijah will come before the day of the Lord: "He will turn the hearts of the fathers to their children, and the hearts of the children to their fathers; or else I will come and strike the land with a curse" (Mal. 4:6). God desires reconciliation.

Why do good people do bad things? Often they are in reaction (or rebellion) toward their parents, most often their father. Of course, they are personally responsible for their actions, for as adults they cannot say, "My father made me do it." But given the heart's proclivity toward self-determination, some children never do outgrow the effects of bad parenting.

A man who struggles with his sexuality said that when he was a boy, he tried to discuss his feelings with his father but was always rebuffed. Because the father always steered the conversation in another direction, the boy thought that no one—not even his father—could understand or handle his increasing sexual desires. This created both fear and a powerful preoccupation with feelings he thought were extraordinarily strong and different. The one thing that haunts us is the fear that we are different, that no one has ever had our struggles, that no one can understand our secret fascinations. Healthy communication with a father dispels those fears.

After an argument with her father, a sixteen-year-old girl went up to her room and committed suicide with her father's gun. The heartbroken mother told me, "My husband did not grieve. . . . He has not shed a tear. He went to work the day after the funeral as if nothing had ever happened. We can't talk about it." This dear woman must bear the pain alone, for her husband has disengaged his feelings, immune from love, pain, and even pity. Think of how that teenager would feel if she could know that though she died by her own hand, using her father's gun, her demise did not bring a single tear to her father's eye!

Can we be reconciled to our fathers? Yes, even if your father has already died you can make peace with him in your heart. Ernest Hemingway could have chosen a different path despite the apparent insensitivity of his parents. If he had come to know his Father in heaven, he could have endured his disappointments.

THE SEARCH FOR A FATHER'S LOVE

Our society is reeling from the effects of absentee fathers in our homes. About 40 percent of the children in this country live in a home without their fathers, and more than 50 percent face unresolved problems with their fathers. Statistics indicate that in excess of 70 percent of prisoners come from families in which the father was absent.[4]

We must try to feel the pain of those children whose fathers abandoned them. Even contemporary songs sometimes speak of the emptiness of knowing that the one who gave the child a name—the one who gave life—then walked away. Whether one is physically or emotionally abandoned, the result is the same: a feeling of worthlessness, hopelessness, and rejection. In the next chapter we will discover that often those who struggle with addictions suffer from what one counselor calls a "father wound" in their souls.

As we know, the moment we are born we begin to pursue significance. We have a desire to mean something to somebody. If you were reared in a home in which you had the two ingredients of love and respect, you will feel significant; you will feel as if you matter. And your father has the power to confer that significance, as well as the power to steal it from you. His acceptance will enrich you; his rejection will diminish you.

When a father rejects a child, the message received is, "He does not love me because I am unlovable; I am defective and at core unfixable." A father does not have to say the words, of course. All that he has to do is be indifferent, uncaring, or absent and the child will get the message.

Boys reared without a father will have a harder time trying to restrain themselves; they do not know how to balance their natural drives, since they have not seen manhood modeled before them. Such children are more prone to violence, more involved in sexual expression, and more vulnerable to addictions.

Listen to these words, written to me by a grown man: "I haven't had a heart-to-heart talk with my father since I was three years old. We were told we should not have feelings or emotions. We were falsely accused of sexual matters and yet expected to pretend that everything was fine. As an adult I fail at everything; I run from one thing to another, for I fear both failure and success." He adds that his mother now tells him that he should have outgrown his problems. But he can't seem to make up for the years of childhood he missed.

Girls who do not have a father in the home—or who have a father who ignores or abuses them—are more likely to become sexually active at a younger age. They are less likely to have healthy relationships with men. We've all known young women who have said that they moved in with a boyfriend or married at an early age just to escape from home. They don't know whether they are lovable or not, so they fall into the arms of the first boy who says, "I love you." They do not realize that what he means is, "I love myself; I want you." When that relationship ends, the young woman will look for another man and then another, always craving male affirmation.

The owner of a strip joint in Chicago said, "These girls are dancing for the fathers they did not have." In effect, they are crying, "Father, don't you see how beautiful I am?" They are prey to the most vile men, for their need to be affirmed by a man is insatiable; they desire attention and approval even if they have to strip for it. One of them said, "Yes, we are here for the money, but more than that we are looking for affirmation; we are trying to find someone who actually believes we are beautiful."

A young woman whose father called her a "whore" if her skirts were too short now struggles with her relationship with her boyfriend. No matter how kind he is to her, she becomes angry and wants to "crush him" for his kindnesses. In a letter she wrote, "As soon as I think my father's influence over my thoughts has been erased, he somehow comes creeping back to torment me." Having been devalued in the eyes of her father, she believes that any genuine love a man might show to her is misplaced. She wants him to treat her as she thinks she deserves to be treated, namely, abusively.

The late Princess Diana grew up in a home in which her parents divorced, and so she felt rejected. When her father dropped her off at a boarding school she screamed, "If you leave me here, I will hate you for the rest of my life." Patrick Jephson, who was her assistant for eight years and knew her as well as anyone, wrote that she was manipulative and unstable and "avidly consumed what men offered and threw them away like an empty husk."[5]

Of course none of us can appreciate the pressure Diana was under, given the expectations that the world had for her and Prince Charles. But Jephson added, "Her need for attention was all-consuming and few people could produce the affirmation in quantities required. . . . She never did find the love she wanted in this world."[6] Having felt rejected and abandoned, she inherited insecurities that the fame and adjuration of the world could not fill. When such people marry, they are a bottomless pit of unmet needs. Because they see themselves as fundamentally unlovable, no amount of love and attention can give them the solid sense of security they seek.

A child's relationship to his/her father is the strongest predictor of the child's later success or failure with school and friends. According to a long-term study at Harvard University, children who grew up with a healthy relationship to their father grew up with more compassion, better social relationships, and happier marriages.[7]

Fathering has always been dear to God's heart, since fathering is designed to be the foundation of society. God is the original Father. There are 1,180 references to *father* in the Bible (in comparison to 324 for *mother*). The father is to exercise leadership, authority, and honor. The influence of a father is to last for generations. And God will either reward or judge fathers on the basis of how they rear their children.

We must be at peace with both our fathers, the heavenly and the earthly.

AT PEACE WITH OUR HEAVENLY FATHER

Why are so many people not free, haunted by a father who did not love them? Why do so many people have a bottomless pit of unmet needs because of the failures of their parents? Why do we talk about the love of God and still remain stone-cold in our hearts? Why is our faith intellectual, often devoid of emotion—devoid of joy, for example?

In his book *Abba's Child*, Brennan Manning says that we are not free to enjoy our relationship with our heavenly Father because we think that He feels about us the way we feel about ourselves. We feel sinful, disgusted, and we think that God is disgusted and vengeful. We cannot accept His love; we can't rejoice in it because we are bound in our own sinful self. But feelings are not facts.[8] Manning gives other reasons for our emptiness.

Also, we have been taught to be dishonest about our emotions. Those who are reared in a dysfunctional home where they were not permitted to feel but had to keep their emotions bottled in their souls—the grown children who had no place to cry—find it particularly difficult to trust in God and enjoy His love. They had to fall in line in their homes like robots, and they go through the same routine in their relationship with God.

We have to stop lying about our loneliness, our guilt, our fears and insecurities, and our sense of disappointment in other people. We must stop trying to project an air of religiosity that masks an empty life. We must get over the idea that how we appear to others is what is most important. We must begin with honesty toward God; and if we begin there, we shall find it easier to be honest before others. We don't experience reality until we ourselves are real (honest).

In addition, we think that God's love is dependent on our performance, and that keeps us bound, unable to experience Him. We do not enjoy Him, for we are forever falling short, disappointing ourselves and Him, too. We do not allow God to love us as we are; we still think we have to make ourselves worthy of grace, worthy of His love and blessing. So we are both driven and unfulfilled. Driven because we know that we are not meeting expectations and unfulfilled because no matter how hard we try we are driven to try harder.

Manning asks us to ponder this question: Suppose you greatly sinned this coming week (though I pray you won't), what would you do? Would you be drawn away from Christ because of your shame and regret, or would you hurry in His direction, running into His wide-open arms? If we say, "I must run away, for I cannot come to the One whom I have displeased," then, of course, it shows that we are stuck in the performance rut; we forget that we are loved as the Father loves Christ, on the basis of Christ, not our successes or failures.[9] We must give ourselves permission to experience God's love.

Accept His Love

Yes, we must spill our hearts out to God and let Him love us. His love is to be experienced, for it is love that "surpasses knowledge," and through it we are "filled to the measure of all the fullness of God" (Eph. 3:19). We are too tightly wound; we must accept His love into our hearts. We forget that God loves us though we are unworthy, though we are without strength; He loves us even when we don't love Him in return. Because we do not have to make ourselves worthy for God to love us, we would be greatly freed if we shed the mask of our false self and enjoyed authentic honesty in His presence and the presence of others.

Yes, God is a God of judgment, but my experience has been that it is easier to believe in the judgment of God than the grace of God; it is easier to believe that He will discipline us than to believe that He will unconditionally love us. And most of us are in need of love in great quantities. God makes no distinction between the love He has for His beloved Son and the love He has for us (see John 17:23). Do you realize it would be heresy to say that God would love you more if only you were better! His love is not dependent on your performance. Yes, He is displeased with us when we disobey, but His love is unchangeable. He will not abandon us or put us up for adoption.

When our daughters were born, my wife and I did not say to ourselves that we would wait until we saw how well they performed before we loved them. If the eldest becomes a nurse, the second a teacher, and the third a missionary—then we will really love them! No, we loved them before they were born; their only qualification was that they be born to us. We loved them because we loved them.

Our heavenly Father chose us from before the foundation of the world, long before we had any opportunity to love in return. He loves us because we are His children. "How great is the love the Father has lavished on us" (1 John 3:1). If we could better grasp His love, we would be less concerned about the failures of our parents. The One whose opinion matters the most and knows us the best, loves us!

Just as we have the natures of our earthly fathers, so we have been begotten by our heavenly Father, who has implanted His life in us. Just as in human birth the egg and the sperm unite to form human life, so God takes the Spirit of God and combines it with the Word of God to produce the life of God. We are "partakers of the divine nature." In fact, there is a part of us that cannot sin (see 1 John 3:9). Sin is responsible for death; God is responsible for life.

But how can we trust our heavenly Father when it seems so obvious that He does not give us the same care as most earthly fathers? For example, I know that my father would keep me from having cancer if it were within his power to do so; he would keep me from accidents, heartaches, and disappointments if all power were in his hand. But the actions of our heavenly Father are less predictable; He allows (plans?) the most heartbreaking of circumstances. Does He really love us?

The answer is yes, He does love us—even more than an earthly father could. But He has a different agenda. Our earthly father values our comfort; our heavenly Father values our faith. Our earthly father values happiness; our heavenly Father values holiness. Our earthly father values the blessings of time; our heavenly Father values the blessings of eternity. This is why Paul wrote, "I consider that our present sufferings are not worth comparing with the glory that will be revealed in us" (Rom. 8:18).

No matter what our trials are, in the end we shall be exalted to sit with His Son on the throne of the universe: "To him who overcomes, I will give the right to sit with me on my throne, just as I overcame and sat down with my Father on his throne" (Rev. 3:21). Here at last we see the epitome of divine grace, as the Father delights in those whom He has adopted.

Fathers reproduce after their kind. The older I get, the more I look like my earthly father; just so the longer I walk in the Christian life, the more I should resemble my heavenly Father. "Be imitators of God, therefore, as dearly loved children and live a life of love, just as Christ loved us and gave himself up for us as a fragrant offering and sacrifice to God" (Eph. 5:1–2).

Those who have been rejected by their earthly fathers have a safe place to weep before the Lord; they can open their lives to Him and enjoy His company. In His presence, they can be honest, knowing they will be received. Hemingway would not have had to commit suicide. Whatever disappointment he experienced with his parents and the church, he could have received the blessing of their God. He could have taken refuge in his Father in heaven, for "the name of the LORD is a strong tower; the righteous run to it and are safe" (Prov. 18:10).

When we are at peace with our heavenly Father, we are better prepared to make peace with our earthly father. Having been forgiven much, we are now ready to forgive.

AT PEACE WITH OUR EARTHLY FATHERS

One woman with an abusive father said that she did not visit his grave "for fear that his hand would come out of the earth to hit me one more time." How can she make peace with her father without his cooperation? Can there be peace without reconciliation, and without an accounting of what has happened? Thankfully, the answer is *yes*.

Those whose fathers either physically or verbally abused them, or abandoned them, have a past that needs to be faced. They must be willing to identify what happened and mourn that part of their lives that was lost to them. In fact, it is beneficial for such children to visualize what the past might have been so that they can fully appreciate what they missed, for grief is the way that we adapt to the loss.

In his excellent book *Making Peace with Your Father,* David Stoop, speaking to those who have had bad parenting, says, "To a large extent, making peace with our father is a matter of working our way through the grieving process."[10] And, when people avoid expressing anger over their losses, the grieving process "gets stuck." The good news is that whether one's father is dead or alive, it is possible to make peace with him. Whether or not we will still be controlled by our past is really up to us. The decisions we make will determine the direction of our lives.

After a period of understanding and waiting, it is time to forgive. This, of course, is more difficult for some than for others, because of either temperament or the severity of rejection or abuse. Our desire that God administer justice is right and proper; however, we must be willing to entrust that into His hands, even as Jesus did (see 1 Pet. 2:23). In this life we cannot "even the score"; we must leave that to the Judge of the universe.

Keep in mind that forgiving someone does not mean that we condone his/her behavior. Nor does it mean pretending nothing happened or diminishing the severity of the offense. God has forgiven us, not by minimizing our sin, but by taking the full consequences upon Himself in the person of Christ. Forgiveness is free to the one who receives it but costly to the one who grants it. Our salvation cost God plenty, and now we are commanded, "Be kind and compassionate to one another, forgiving each other, just as in Christ God forgave you" (Eph. 4:32).

Thankfully, forgiveness is not the same as reconciliation; for many who read this book, reconciliation is impossible, either because the father does not acknowledge his wrongs or because he has already died. To quote Stoop again, "Reconciliation is bilateral: It is something both parties must do together. If you have hurt me, and we are estranged as a result, I can forgive you on my own without your permission, without your even knowing about it."[11] Reconciliation is ideal, but if it is impossible, forgiveness can still be granted. In other words, your father need no longer destroy your life through bitterness. You can forgive and be set free.

Forgiveness is both an act and a process. You might forgive the drunken motorist who asks for forgiveness for running over your foot, but you dare not think that that will heal your crushed toes. In fact, despite your pronouncement of forgiveness, you might find anger and bitterness in your heart in the weeks to come. But you have chosen to forgive, so you maintain the stance of forgiveness, refusing to allow the bitterness back into your heart. Having chosen to forgive, you keep forgiving until the power of the anger and bitterness subsides.

We must never think that we have to wait until we feel like forgiving before we do so. Forgiveness is a choice, not an emotion. Forgiveness is what God gives us the grace to do, though we don't feel like it. Thousands of people who have been the victims of bad parenting say that their past is no longer an issue because they have laid it to rest. You can do the same. If you are haunted by your past, begin by saying these words: "In the name of Jesus, I choose to forgive."

HELD TO THE FATHER'S HEART

In his book *Abba's Child,* Brennan Manning tells the story of a Jewish boy named Mordecai who defied his parents and would not attend the synagogue.[12] All that he wanted to do was to go into the woods and enjoy God's creation. They tried to cure him with behavior modification experts, who modified his behavior until there was nothing left to be modified. They called in the psychoanalysts to unblock his blockages until there was nothing left to unblock. There seemed to be no hope.

Finally, a great rabbi visited the village and they told him their tale of woe. He just said, "Leave the boy with me." When the parents left, he said nothing but took the boy and held him silently against his heart.

And the next day, the boy went to the synagogue and then to the woods, where he spoke the words of God. And he grew up to be a great man, and when people were seized in panic, they came to him and found peace. And he said, "I first learned the Word of God when the great rabbi held me silently against his heart."

The heart is understood as the locus of the emotions from which strong feelings of love and hatred arise. It is the symbol we employ when we capture the deepest essence of personhood; it symbolizes what lies at the core of our being. When the boy was held against the rabbi's heart, he penetrated the rabbi's consciousness and came to know him in a way that embraced not only the intellect but also the emotion. Heart spoke to heart.

Manning makes this application: If you would have asked John the Apostle, "Who are you?" he would not have said, "The author of the fourth Gospel." Nor would he have said, "I am the author of the Epistles of John" or "I was a disciple of Jesus." No, that was not his identity.

Who was he? He defined himself as "the disciple whom Jesus loved" and "the one who leaned on His breast at dinner." He was at the breast of Jesus, and that for him was all that he needed.

We are not healed from our hurts as long as our identity is lawyer, doctor, carpenter, bricklayer, or preacher. We are healed only when we are the child whom God loves, the one who rests in His unconditional passionate love toward us, despite our feelings and our sins.

We are loved because we are loved.

Cleland McAfee wrote:

There is a place of quiet rest, near to the heart of God
A place where sin cannot molest, near to the heart of God
O, Jesus, blest redeemer sent from the heart of God.
Hold us who wait before thee, near to the heart of God.

Ernest Hemingway could have known that rest and that love. How different it all could have been if he had turned to the One who heals our souls.

A Promise to Ponder

Though my father and mother forsake me, the LORD will receive me.

—Ps. 27:10

CHAPTER 8
THE PATH TO ADDICTION

THERE IS A STORY about a crack cocaine addict in New York who chained himself to a radiator so that he would not be able to leave his room to get another fix. But, in desperation, he was able to break loose the radiator with his free hand; then he carried the piece of metal down the stairs and into the street so he could get high once more. He explained, "Cocaine has a voice, and when it calls, I must obey."

Addicts of all kinds have heard that voice and have obeyed. Some have heard the voice of alcoholism; others, the voice of gambling, pornography, or sexual exploits. They wonder how they could have fallen so far, so fast; and they also wonder whether it is possible to be free. If only they could turn a deaf ear when that voice calls.

We've already learned that we are, for the most part, desire driven. The sensations of the body are much more present to us than the rational considerations of the soul. A sex addict put it this way: "I sought more outrageous, violent, and anonymous sex, and each time the present moment was so powerful that I couldn't even think about the consequences." But, as he learned, consequences come whether we think about them or not.

Most addicts must, of necessity, live in denial; they are incapable of honesty. They cannot admit to themselves that their lives and the lives of those around them are being destroyed. The child molester tells himself that he is not hurting children; the alcoholic tells himself that he is not destroying his family; and the gambler tells himself that, given enough time, he will earn his lost money back. And if an addict is able to abstain from his addiction for a time, he will delude himself into believing that he is in control.

Earlier in this book we were introduced to the crafty art of "double-think," that is, the ability to hold contradictory beliefs in one's mind simultaneously and accept both of them. On the one hand addicts know that what they are doing is wrong; on the other, they keep telling themselves that their desires deserve to be satisfied and that they can minimize the consequences of their actions. They hear the voice of their addiction but are deaf to the pleading of friends and family.

The sobering fact is that the basis for addiction resides in all of us! It is found in the normal desire we have to avoid pain and maximize happiness. If we ask why good people do bad things—why addictions develop in children from fine homes and good churches, why people with good jobs and healthy relationships end up as addicts—there is only one answer: *An addiction is an illusionary promise to avoid pain by creating a way of escape into the world of pleasurable sensations.*

We must approach this subject with two cautions. First, we must not be unduly judgmental, since any one of us, given the right conditions, could have entered the path of addiction. Second, we must not see an addiction as a disease for which the addict has no responsibility. We don't hold a person responsible for having arthritis, but we do know that unless the addict accepts responsibility there is no hope for his recovery. Addictions are rooted in a wrong theology.

In the Book of Romans, Paul gives the spiritual history of the human race, detailing the origins of sexual immorality and the like. In the process he shows that the history of the race is really the history of individuals: Civilizations follow well-worn paths to destruction, but so do human beings. The cycle of sin begins when we think wrongly about God.

We read in part:

> For although they knew God, they neither glorified him as God nor gave thanks to him, but their thinking became futile and their

foolish hearts were darkened. Although they claimed to be wise, they became fools and exchanged the glory of the immortal God for images made to look like mortal man and birds and animals and reptiles.

Therefore God gave them over in the sinful desires of their hearts to sexual impurity for the degrading of their bodies with one another. They exchanged the truth of God for a lie, and worshiped and served created things rather than the Creator—who is forever praised. Amen.

Because of this, God gave them over to shameful lusts. (Rom. 1:21–26)

God gave them over to shameful lusts! What a description of addicts! Without restraint, often without remorse, and seemingly without the ability to repent, addicts march obediently down the long road to moral and spiritual destruction. Let's retrace the steps of those whose lives have spun out of control by what one writer calls "the blinding self-absorption of sin."

Thankfully, all is not lost. The same God who gives people over to their shameful lusts is the One who delivers them when they cry to Him. While most addicts die as slaves to their addiction, hundreds of thousands have proved that there is hope even for those who have fallen the farthest. But before we learn about freedom from the chains of addition, let us think through the description we have just read.

OUT OF CONTROL

Paul says that the members of society have exchanged wisdom for foolishness: "Although they claimed to be wise, they became fools." Glance across the spiritual landscape of America today and you will agree that, for the most part, society believes that biblical morality is primitive, outmoded, and otherwise, the possession of fools. The "enlightened" can enjoy alcohol and sensual pleasures and live by their own rules.

They believe that God, if He exists at all, has the responsibility of affirming their deepest cravings. But it is precisely those cravings that are the pathway to addiction. And, sadly, even those of us who believe in the one true God can follow the lead of our desires and be ruled by them.

Nations and families have an interconnectedness, a solidarity, if you please, that affects one generation after another. There is little doubt that we have more addictions today because our society as a whole has lost its restraints and changed its view of God. And with the breakup of the family, we have more children reared with unmet needs, and more opportunities to meet those needs with the many addictions that are easily available.

Second, they "exchanged the truth of God" for a lie. As spiritual creatures, we can't live without seeking that which is beyond us. A man trying to live without a god is like a fish trying to live without water. Therefore, when the truth is abandoned, a false god is worshiped. The people Paul described stopped believing that God was good, so we read, "they did not give thanks." That is, they took God's blessings for granted and thought they deserved more. The result was that they abandoned the true God for one of their own making.

We will never understand the power of addiction unless we realize that the substance to which people are addicted makes all the same promises God makes. The alcoholic believes that his drink is more dependable than God. For one thing, it will always give him that euphoria that will deliver him from the pain of reality. Also, this "god" will perform on command. No matter how difficult life gets, the substance responds whenever he wants it to. Friends may fail him, his family will desert him, but his precious bottle will always be there. Addiction is idolatry of the worst sort.

Addicts' worship of the things of this world—which is really a worship of themselves—now becomes all-consuming. God is blocked out of their lives, and they are free to pursue their own self-protective measures by blocking out the pain and guilt. Thus, their sin causes them to plunge into more sin, to become more self-absorbed and bound by the dictates of fleshly desires.

Paul explains more fully, "They changed the truth of God into a lie." The lie is simply this: I have both the right and the ability to meet my own needs as I see fit. I will be the judge as to what path leads to happiness, and I will do as I please. Rather than loving the Lord my God "with all my heart, mind, and soul," I will love myself and serve my own perceived interests first. Sin says, "This way to happiness," but in the end it stings and damns.

The other side of the lie is that though I suspect my behavior is going in the wrong direction, I will not listen to the voice of conscience or the warnings of reason, but will be driven by my own desires. The addict wills to be ignorant of the consequences of his lifestyle, and besides, he's not hurting anyone. The medieval theologian Thomas Aquinas observed that "ignorance is sometimes directly and intrinsically voluntary, as when one freely chooses to be ignorant so that he may sin more freely."[1] Thus addicts act against their better judgment and choose ignorance to avoid the agony of repentance.

Here again, the impact of the family is enormous. A child reared in an abusive, alcoholic home will either react against his upbringing and become a teetotaler or reproduce the sins of his parents, following them in their addiction. A child who has been molested will find it difficult to maintain sexual boundaries and may be open to sexual addictions. Think also of the child reared in the ghetto where drugs are freely available and the peer pressure is strong. All of these factors contribute to the behavioral patterns of the child, who will take his core beliefs into adulthood.

A child reared in a home with a warped conception of God, with parents who themselves are driven by their desires, is going to find it more difficult to restrain his impulses. Many of these children think they are powerless to say no to a life of self-indulgence, though they know its ugly consequences. Almost always, the roots of addiction lie within the home, thanks to the impact of parents and the basic solidarity of our close-knit relationships. Patrick Carnes perceptively notes, "Sexual compulsiveness, like all addictions, rests in a complex web of family relationships."[2]

For the addict, the motivation is to maintain a positive image, no matter the cost. Since someone has to be responsible for losing a job, for example, and it cannot be the addict (for he believes his lies), the blame must be shifted to someone else. This shield of denial enables him to mitigate the full impact of shame and guilt and to anticipate objections to his lifestyle that will come either from his own conscience or from others. He will build a world in his imagination that will be a refuge from the real world. He will move back and forth so cleverly that no one will probably notice it.

Once the addict begins to believe his lies, his lifestyle seems irreversible; that is, he has invested so much in his excuses, he has endured so much reproach from his family, he has already felt so many bitter consequences of his behavior that he believes he deserves his bit of pleasure, no matter what others think. Coming to the light of truth appears not only too costly, but quite impossible. Having boarded the train, the addict must now take it all the way to the station.

THE ADDICTIVE PERSONALITY

We've already learned that at its most basic level, addiction "is an attempt to control and fulfill the desire for happiness."[3] Addiction is a search for happiness and meaning that has run amuck. Every addict engages in a relationship with an object or event to produce a change of mood, a euphoric experience that promises escape from boredom, inner loneliness, and pain.

Indeed, this trance makes the addict detached from his surroundings; he lives in two worlds, the world of reality and the world of addiction. And when reality becomes too depressing, he can escape into his private world with sensual excitement and, believe it or not, a feeling of control. Just the anticipation stimulates him; life without these sensations seems unbearable. He spends a great deal of time making sure that nothing will ever come between him and this beautiful feeling.

We cannot understand the addict unless we understand the change of mood, the euphoria, that his substance or activity brings. The whole life of the addict is focused on his ability to create this ecstasy, an inner feeling of sensual excitement. One telltale sign is a rapid heartbeat as he anticipates the moment when his desires will be fulfilled. For the voyeur, just the suspense of looking into a neighbor's window with the hope of seeing a glimpse of nudity is sufficient to give him a rush. The alcoholic who binges on Friday night already feels the euphoria on Thursday as he thinks about tomorrow evening.

The addict believes he has found an activity that will provide this euphoric experience on cue. His friends have failed him, his family does not understand, his employer has been harsh, but he can have a euphoric experience whenever he wills it. Not even the Almighty guarantees this kind of instant gratification. This secret world will become more real to him than his public life, even as he struggles to present an image of normalcy to the outside world. But this mood change is the common denominator of addictions. Consider:

- The shoplifter's heart beats wildly with excitement while stealing clothes from a department store.
- The sex addict experiences a sensual mood change while looking at pornography or planning a sexual tryst.
- The shopaholic experiences a sense of excitement and control while on a spending spree.
- The gambler is almost in a trance when he makes a major bet on his favorite football team.
- The drug addict has a euphoric sensation as he holds money in his hand to purchase his favorite substance.
- The serial killer is worked into an erotic lather as he methodically plans his crimes and visualizes their execution.
- The alcoholic coming off his hangover can already feel the ecstasy as he anticipates his next binge.
- The arsonist has erotic stimulation as he sees a burning building for which he is responsible.

And to think, these feelings can be repeated on command! The addict knows that if he has the money, combined with the opportunity, he can re-create these powerful sensations. Though his life is out of control, he tells himself that he himself is in control, capable of escaping into this world of uninhibited pleasure and euphoric eroticism. He thinks that no one else has ever experienced the intense pleasure he receives through his addiction. He feels literally "taken over" by desires he does not fully understand.

The problem, of course, is that the substance does not keep its promises. The high fades away, the trance subsides. The addict is left with his pain, plus increased guilt and shame. What is more, he now experiences the law of diminishing returns: That which at one time sent him into his private world of ecstasy no longer excites him. To re-create the same effect, he must increase the dosage or increase the risk. The sex addict must opt for more bizarre exploits. The alcoholic must drink more and more and must now drink to solve the problems his drinking caused. The gambler must take greater risks. As the inflamed desires increase, so do the pain, guilt, and emptiness.

Within time, the addict becomes cunning and manipulative and will exploit anyone with whom he has contact. For one thing, he needs money, so he will become a master at using guilt, threats, false accusations, intimidation, pleading, promises of reform, and the like—all with the intention of protecting himself and his habit. Just when you think that you have heard and seen it all, he will come up with a devious scheme that baffles the imagination. And, surprisingly, he will often get what he wants.

Does he not care about his family? He tells himself that he does, but the truth is that he does not. He sees them only in relation to one question: How can they be used to protect my addiction? They will be expected to lie for him, to give him money, to try to see his viewpoint. He will shift blame for his problems onto their shoulders with manipulation and guilt. People, like his substance, are to be used to help him accomplish his ends. He retreats into his inner world, withdrawing from all meaningful relationships. His obsession replaces the people in his life. He closes off all avenues of vulnerability in communication.

Delusion

Read this description of an addict's delusion:

> *Sincere delusion* is believing your own lies. The addicts who make a
> commitment to change or follow through on something are insin-
> cere in their intentions. They are as sincere as when they vow to
> themselves to quit. They may experience a great deal of emotion—
> tears of pain, expressions of tenderness, or anger when someone
> does not believe their good intentions. However, their commit-
> ment to others is no more valid than their vows to themselves. It
> appears to be paradoxical to be sincere about telling a lie. It is not.
> But it is evidence of seriously impaired thinking.[4]

If the addict is able to stop his addiction for a time, he tells himself
he is not a addict after all, since he has just proved that he is in control.
(I'm reminded of Mark Twain's telling remark, "Of course I can quit
smoking; I've quit a thousand times!") Of course he does not quit but
after a time returns to his deceptive and destructive behavior. Deeper
and deeper he sinks into denial and into his delusional world.

His appearance of sincerity only further insulates him from reality.
He tells himself that his addiction is not really a part of who he is, that
deep down he really is caring, loving, and the like. He tells himself that
given all the injustices of life, he deserves this bit of pleasure. He tells
himself that his habit does not hurt anyone. His problem is ungrateful
children, a demanding spouse, unrealistic expectations at work, or the
hypocrisy of the church members.

Keep in mind that deep inside he also wants acceptance from other
people. So, there are times when he will be kind, charming, and generous,
trying to "buy" a sense of respect and friendship. This only gives false hope
to those who live with him; they think that this time he is going to change,
but as we have learned, he underestimates the extent of his problem and
overestimates his abilities. All of this gives him one more opportunity to
believe his illusions. He has not yet admitted the truth to himself.

An addiction can change a person's personality for the rest of his life. Apart from a radical transformation, he will never see reality as it really is. All of life will be interpreted through the grid of his twisted experience; in one way or another he will reflect the skewed logic he uses so convincingly. He will tend to divide the human race into two categories, those who agree with him (friends) and those who don't see life his way (enemies). His view of money, relationships, and God—all of these will be viewed through his addictive lens.

CHAINS THAT HOLD THE ADDICT BOUND

The question, of course, is: Why doesn't the addict simply walk away from his addiction? Does he not see that it is destroying him and those around him? Surely, he knows, underneath all the denial, that this behavior is self-destructive. Why does he not, with a heroic act of the will, say, "Enough is enough" and never touch his substance or repeat his destructive behavior again? We read in Proverbs, "For a man's ways are in full view of the LORD, and he examines all his paths. The evil deeds of a wicked man ensnare him; the cords of his sin hold him fast. He will die for lack of discipline, led astray by his own great folly" (Prov. 5:22–23). *The cords of his sin hold him fast!*

What might these "cords" be that will not let the addict go free?

Escape

First and foremost is the mood change we have already described. The thought of living with raw pain and self-condemning emptiness is more than he can bear. Living with his true feelings, trying to reestablish proper patterns of behavior, and rectifying destroyed personal relationships simply appear to be beyond the realm of possibility. One addict described it this way to me: "To be asked to change was equivalent to being asked to lift a building with my bare hands. Unthinkable." The addict's only escape is to re-create the waves of sensation that pulse through his body.

Guilt and Shame

Second, there are guilt and shame. Much as the addict might deny that he is doing anything shameful, the very fact that he usually tries to hide his practice is proof enough that he feels the sting of self-condemnation. Imagine the energy that will go into managing the conscience, trying to deaden its persistent voice. No wonder he needs his addiction to live with himself.

By now the addict has already been condemned by those whom he professed to love. His family looks upon him with disgust; his relatives have only polite, cursory contact with him; the people at work glance the other way when he walks into the room. Whether or not words are spoken makes little difference. The addict believes that people are rejecting him. He thinks that everyone he meets can see right through him, down to the phoniness of his public persona. If he were to "come clean" and admit to his great need, no one could possibly love him or think he was worthy of redemption. Thus the shame remains trapped inside, to be silenced only by the addiction that controls him.

Secrecy

Third, there is secrecy. Even when the addiction is known to those who are close to him, the addict believes that no one has ever had his experiences, and therefore no one can truly understand him. So his addiction is something that cannot be talked about. He will meticulously hide his behavior from those who do not know, always trying to maintain that veneer of normalcy. He knows that it is not his true self, yet the fiction must be maintained at all costs.

Along with this is the fear of rejection. There are moments when the addict wants help and might actually plan to break his silence, but he believes that he would encounter nothing but judgmental attitudes, devoid of understanding and sympathy. He keenly feels the emotional need to be accepted and loved, but his addiction has hurt so many others that reconciliation seems impossible. He has burned his bridges, so he might just as well retreat within himself and accept his hopelessness. So, though he lives with others, he lives alone, isolated in his small world.

He is between the proverbial rock and a hard place. If he tells his story, he fears rejection; yet the only way for him to get out of his prison is to share his need with another human being. He wants to be free of his addiction, yet he cannot imagine life without it. He prefers to be able to control his addiction, but the addiction controls him.

When his inner pain appears to be unbearable, the addict might resort to violent behavior. Physical violence and outbursts of temper are escape valves for his emptiness and frustration. No matter where he looks, he sees nothing but despair. At this point, some addicts commit suicide, but others finally give up and surrender their lives to the God who has been waiting in the shadows.

FREE AT LAST

As always, we can be sure that the truth sets people free. Reality will have to be faced; the grim truth of addiction will have to be admitted. Both the extent of his problem and the helplessness of his own solutions will have to be acknowledged. *For only when the part that has been denied is finally admitted can healing take place.*

Carnes writes, "A moment comes for every addict when the consequences are so great or the pain is so bad that the addict admits that life is out of control."[5] No doubt most addicts have had many such "moments," only to make new resolutions and then return to the addiction. But yes, there are times when the addict is finally ready to pay the price of honesty and vulnerability—no matter what. Hopefully, when he has reached the bottom, he will look up to God.

Does this mean there is nothing we can do to help the addict but watch him destroy himself, waiting for him to "hit bottom"? Thankfully, the bottom can be raised so that he can hit it before everything is destroyed. Counselors have discovered that those who are closest to the addict (usually family members) can intervene to help him see the full extent of his need, so that he can seek help before it is too late. As loved ones share about how the addiction has affected them personally, reality might dawn. In other words, the sooner the addict is brought to admit to the deceits in his heart, the better.

These matters are never simple. If one parent is an addict, the addiction must be treated as part of the whole network of family relationships, for every member has been severely affected. Remember, there is no such thing as an addict who lives in isolation: No one lives unto himself or dies unto himself, but our behavior affects a whole web of relationships.

Many self-help groups have enabled addicts to get in touch with their feelings and reality. Alcoholics Anonymous, Gamblers Anonymous, and other such groups have a measure of success because they provide an environment where people with similar struggles can be honest, open, and caring with one another. In such an atmosphere, there are accountability and strong peer pressure to change behavioral patterns. However, a change in behavior is not the same as a change in desires.

When God becomes a part of the deliverance process, and when Christ becomes the means into His presence, there is a shaking of one's core beliefs about forgiveness, self-perception, and the possibility of transformation. These beliefs can become the basis for a whole new lens through which the addict can see his own life and the world around him. We must, of course, ruefully admit that even those who have experienced the reconciling power of Christ can still be ensnared in one addiction or another. Not a one of us is guaranteed immunity from the serious consequences of sin. But deliverance is possible through Christ because provision has been made for it.

I do not understand why some people experience instant deliverance by Christ's power and others do not. We've all heard many stories of men who have poured out their last bottle of alcohol, never to touch it again. I've known cocaine and heroin addicts who quit using drugs cold turkey once they were converted, seeing Christ and themselves in the new light of the gospel. But I've also worked with those who, though soundly converted, still revert back to their former lifestyles, particularly in times of discouragement and stress. There is no neat series of steps that the addict can take to be set free. I list these, not because the order is critical, nor because everyone goes through the same process, but because these are the essentials in any path toward freedom.

Honesty

As we have learned, the first step is honesty. There must be a complete admission of helplessness, the recognition that all of the promises to reform and the deceptive patterns of behavior must come to an end. The lies that have been both lived and told must be admitted; the ugly rationalizations must be exposed for what they are. The more thorough the confession, the greater the chance of healing.

The good news is that because Jesus died on the Cross for sinners, He liberates believers from the guilt of sin—including the guilt and shame of addictions. And those who accept this gospel also have the right to be free from the nagging shame of conscience and self-condemnation. Paul wrote, "Who will bring any charge against those whom God has chosen? It is God who justifies. Who is he that condemns? Christ Jesus, who died—more than that, who was raised to life—is at the right hand of God and is also interceding for us" (Rom. 8:33–34).

Having received this gift of eternal life, we now have the right to a clear conscience. For "if we confess our sins, He is faithful and righteous to forgive us our sins and to cleanse us from all unrighteousness" (1 John 1:9 NASB). Not only are we forgiven through confession, but we are also cleansed; that is, our conscience no longer accuses us. And we can forgive ourselves because the God of the universe has forgiven us.

New in Christ

Second, because the addict's perception of himself will dictate his behavior, he must see himself, not as the liar he once was—not as the self-absorbed destroyer that is a part of his legacy—but as one who has been made new in Christ and one who is radically loved by God. He must be taught that God accepts those who come to Him through Christ, not on the basis of performance, but on the basis of undeserved grace. If the addict thinks that God is so angry with him that his case is hopeless, then his case will be as hopeless as he believes it to be. Dozens of verses of Scripture can be memorized and used to show that those whom God accepts through His Son are simply loved because they are loved.

For years the addict has been listening to messages such as: "I am fatally flawed; I am unworthy of love; no one will ever trust me again; there is no hope for me; I deserve to die." Those messages simply perpetuate his own destructive behavior. In Christ we are given a new identity, a new way of seeing ourselves and the world. But these ideas are not easy for an addict to accept. It might take weeks or months before he has the personal assurance that he is indeed loved, cared for by the Father. He does not have to collapse into hopelessness, for he has come to rest in the "God of hope." Let the recovering addict bask in the love God has for even the most decadent sinners. Since God has already saved the worst of sinners, it is not impossible for God to save the worst of addicts (see 1 Tim. 1:15). The addict has to learn that there is nothing he must bring to God except his sick self.

Relationships

Third, he must become part of a caring community. Relationships must be restored. Remember that one of the most powerful chains that holds an addict bound is the fear of rejection, the deeply held belief that if anyone really knew him as he is, he would be condemned, tossed aside. If, when trying to mend past relationships, all he receives is judgment, his fear will have been realized. Thus, the need for genuine acceptance is necessary. Wholeness comes when we are loved in spite of ourselves.

When I lived on a farm we had a horse that wandered off and got stuck in a slough. We had to tie a rope around him and pull him out with the tractor. He got into the mud alone, but he could not get out of it alone. Just so, it is possible to slip into an addiction alone, but it is impossible to get out without the help of others. In the days of his addiction, the addict retreats from open, caring communication and relationships. These must be restored upon release from addiction if he is to have wholeness and accountability. There is no shame in admitting that we need God's help and that of other believers, counselors, or pastors.

One of the metaphors of the church is that of a body with arms and legs and ears and so forth. Like the human body, the body of Christ has within it the capacity to heal itself. Broken bones must be set, but in time they heal. Scars remind us that the gaping wounds have been closed. The recovering addict will most assuredly have to forgive those who have wronged him, just as he asks forgiveness from those he has wronged.

The bottom line is that everything God expects us to do is based on what Christ has already done. Christ crushed sin's power on the Cross; He defeated the enemy of our souls and broke sin's grip. "In the same way, count yourselves dead to sin but alive to God in Christ Jesus. Therefore do not let sin reign in your mortal body so that you obey its evil desires" (Rom. 6:11–12). We can be dressed with the armor of God, so that we can withstand "the devil's schemes" (Eph. 6:11).

A 120-pound woman evicted a 200-pound live-in partner when she went to the police and got a restraining order against him. It was not her strength that did it—it was her authority, her right as the owner of the apartment. To the women who say that they cannot resist the lure of a man, we say, "You can 'stand your ground'" (Eph. 6:13). To the person who says that he is a slave to pornography, we say, "Blessed are the pure in heart, for they will see God" (Matt. 5:8). To the one who is a slave to substance abuse, we say, "So if the Son sets you free, you will be free indeed" (John 8:36).

Why is the struggle so great? God wants us to develop a passion for Christ that is greater than our passion for sin. He can cause us to hate sin and love righteousness. That is the goal toward which He directs us. Thankfully, "where sin increased, grace increased all the more" (Rom.

5:20). Not just the modification of our behavior, but the transformation of our desires is His ultimate goal.

Mel Trotter, who spent years working in a rescue mission to help men overcome their addictions, tells his personal story. Years earlier, when he was an alcoholic, he actually slipped into the funeral home when no one was watching and stole the little shoes from the feet of his dead child, so that he had something to sell to get another drink. When he came into the saving faith of Christ, his life was radically changed, permanently delivered from the addiction. The "voice" of alcohol he had listened to grew silent when he responded to another voice—the message of God's Word.

A PRAYER TO BEGIN THE JOURNEY

If you are praying for an addict, ask God to do what man cannot—to show this person his great need for intervention, both divine and human. Also, realize that our Lord might use you in the process. If you struggle with an addiction, or the affliction of sin, here is a prayer to begin:

> *Father, I thank You that You love me and care about me. I thank You that You know the whole truth about me, all that lies hidden in my soul. You saw me when I was a child; You know all that has become a part of my attitudes, lifestyle, and secret sin.*
>
> *Today, I admit that my sin has not only hurt me and others, but most important, it has grieved You and the blessed Holy Spirit. I deeply repent of my self-deceptions; I admit that I have been dishonest with myself, with others, and even with You.*
>
> *I acknowledge that I am bound in sin and will continue in my addiction unless You help me. Do a mighty work in me and transform my desires.*
>
> *I resist Satan, whose deceptions I have willingly believed. I stand against his carefully laid plans aimed at my destruction.*
>
> *Give me the grace to follow through with any steps of obedience necessary to be wholly free from my enslavement.*

Help me to be subject to all who are in authority within Your church, the body. I pray that You will help me to take my responsibility as a member, to serve You and others as You give me ability.

A Promise to Ponder

For nothing is impossible with God.

—LUKE 1:37

CHAPTER 9
"LET ME CONTROL YOUR LIFE"

Fold *your* jeans double; fold *mine* in thirds."

That was one of dozens of rules a woman demanded her husband follow so that he could be as perfect as she was! She controlled what he ate (and how much); she controlled the use of his discretional time and how he brushed his teeth. He was not to speak until she gave him permission to do so, and she recorded his grade every day. No harm meant of course—"If something is worth doing, it is worth doing right!"

Why do we have this desire to control others? Why this self-willed obsession with our own agenda, our own viewpoint, and confidence in our ability to know what is right for those around us? As we have learned, it all began in Eden when the serpent said to Eve, "You shall be as God, knowing good from evil." Gods, of course, are notorious for wanting to rule. Thus, I rule over my kingdom, you rule over yours, and when our kingdoms collide, there will be conflict. I will plot ways to both protect and expand my kingdom at your expense.

There are levels of control: Some want to control others in personal matters; others want to control those around them to selfishly protect themselves from personal pain or to exalt themselves. For many, controlling other people and circumstances is their only source of personal significance. Some forms of control could be labeled a nuisance, others should be labeled a sin, while some kinds must be called evil. We'll explain in a moment.

Jesus said, "You know that the rulers of the Gentiles lord it over them, and their high officials exercise authority over them. Not so with you. Instead, whoever wants to become great among you must be your servant, and whoever wants to be first must be your slave—just as the Son of Man did not come to be served, but to serve, and to give his life as a ransom for many" (Matt. 20:25–28). The Gentiles (read *pagans*) define greatness in terms of control or power. To rule over a few people is commendable; to rule over many is better. Of course, nations need rulers, and many kings and presidents lead with an attitude of servant leadership, committed to helping their people make things better. But more often than not, leadership is driven by personal ambition and a grandiose quest for power. Thus the adage "Power corrupts, but absolute power corrupts absolutely."

All sin is the exaltation of the self above God; it is the self-will that insists on the control of one's life according to one's own values and desires. And in the process, it involves the control and manipulation of others. Eventually, it will end, for "when a wicked man dies, his hope perishes; all he expected from his power comes to nothing" (Prov. 11:7).

Take any list of sins and at root we find control: We lie to control what people believe; we steal to control what we own; we commit immorality to control what we experience. We scheme to control the outcome of circumstances; we gossip, hoping to control others' reputations. We succumb to various addictions to control our feelings, and we love ourselves more than God so we can control our destiny. Left to ourselves, we are in charge in the worst possible way.

Control is a subtle form of self-exaltation; often it is an obsessive and demonic form of arrogant power. We should not be surprised that controllers often gravitate to churches where they can justify their desire for power with verses of Scripture about the need for others to submit to authority. They are committed to reforming others, but not themselves. Some become the "God told me" controllers who claim to get direct information from the Almighty regarding His plan for their lives and for others. Those who do not submit are defined as rebels fighting against God. Of course, the Bible does speak about submission, but it specifically warns against controlling leadership (see 1 Pet. 5:2–4).

The purpose of this chapter is to describe different kinds of controllers and then ask ourselves what can be done to help us take Jesus' advice seriously: "Whoever wishes to be first among you shall be your slave" (Matt. 20:27 NASB). How do we help those who are obsessed with control, as well as those who have to live with such controllers? No matter how bleak the struggle, there is a message of hope.

CONTROL FREAKS WE HAVE KNOWN

Given the widespread breakdown of our homes, so-called codependent controllers exist everywhere. Think of it this way: If one string of a violin is off-key, then it either has to adjust and get in tune with the other strings, or the other strings will adjust to get in tune with it. Just so, those who live in abusive situations often find themselves adjusting to the atmosphere of the home by wanting to take charge and "fix" the problem. They react against what they see by wanting to be superheroes, rescuers who will try to control the outcome of every situation. Controlling others (for their good, of course!) will now be their obsession.

Determined they will never live in chaos again, these controllers are highly motivated to change themselves and those around them into the kinds of people they want them to be. Their goal, of course, is to minimize the shame and pain associated with their home experiences. But in order to make sure that the future is different from the past, they take charge so that everyone sees the world their way. They have high standards for themselves and expect others to be as perfect as they would like themselves to be. They will lecture, nag, cry, beg, coerce, and use guilt to get people to "shape up." And because any admission of failure on their part exposes their inadequacy and shame, they become defensive and angry when confronted. They find it almost impossible to say, "I was wrong. I'm sorry."

A child brought up by a codependent mother will find her standards impossible to meet. The daughter will be overcorrected, overdisciplined, and overshamed. A child parented in this manner often becomes guilt-ridden and despondent and eventually breaks free from her mother's stringent expectations. The codependent parent berates herself for not having done a good job of parenting and will continue to use guilt to manipulate her wayward child. "How could you do this to *me*, when I've done so much for *you?*" she will ask. What she finds impossible to admit is that part of her child's rebellion is the result of her own parenting. But since the mother feels that she did everything she could to help the child turn out right, she is often incapable of seeing the connection.

Tell a codependent that she is angry and one is met with strong denials. "This has nothing to do with anger; it's a matter of seeing things done right." Or, if she does admit to anger, it is, in her mind, justified. Thus, all attempts to help fail, for the codependent will not give up the fiction that people can be changed with enough shaming, blaming, and nagging. This is an unfortunate kind of perfectionism that eventually ends when the codependent gives up in despair and finally submits her life and circumstances to God.

These perfectionists might be neat freaks, ashamed to be seen unless they are looking their best. They find it very difficult to give compliments because in their view no one really measures up, and those who think they do should be brought down a notch or two. If they overhear a compliment, they will immediately try to "correct it," making sure no one is given high marks. They will tend to exaggerate stories about themselves because of their need to focus on themselves, and they draw their significance from others. As we learned when we studied shame, because these people derive their self-worth from the affirmation of others, they often make excellent caregivers, expending themselves so that they have a sense of fulfillment. Secretly, they want people to notice their hard work and compliment them.

"I Will Control My Body"

Then there are the "I will control my body" controllers. In our discussion about shame, we spoke about those who have eating disorders. They can't control everything around them, but they can control what they eat, even if it kills them. No matter how thin they are, when they look in the mirror they can see only shame; hence, they assume they are overweight. So they starve themselves to death, denying their anger, their inner emptiness, and their single-minded controlling personality.

"Let's Deal with Our Sins"

There is also the "Let's deal with our sins" controller. A promising young Christian man would look for the faults in the girls he dated; he had mastered the art of seeing their weaknesses and had the knack of being able to get them to tell him their personal struggles and sins. Later in the relationship, this information was used as a means of control. He created the fiction that he himself was dealing with sin, too; oh yes, he was not perfect, he allowed, but somehow he was more concerned about his girlfriend's sin than his own. This was the leverage he needed to manipulate and control his girlfriend. To him, the toothpick in someone else's eye was much greater than the beam in his own.

"Let Me Be Your Friend"

Then there is the "Let me be your friend" controller. These people fool us because they are so nice and helpful. In one small country church, a Sunday school teacher would befriend the new pastor, helping him financially and providing free baby-sitting. Later this "kind" man would turn against the pastor, stir up opposition, and force his resignation. This pattern was repeated four times before the elders of the church, who felt intimidated, had the courage to step in and put an end to this control freak's evil ways. Like Diotrephes, a first-century church leader who spread malicious lies about the apostles, this man bolstered his self-esteem through destroying people in ministry (see 3 John 9–10).

A woman smothered a family with gifts and later was enraged when they invited someone else to baby-sit their children. The family didn't realize that the gifts were the price being paid for the privilege of controlling a part of their lives. Free gifts often have a high price.

"Don't Forget, I Am Your Husband"

Let's not overlook the "Don't forget, I am your husband" controller. Yes, husbands are to be heads of their wives; but they are not to control them. Many a man has used the biblical teaching as an excuse for manipulation and strict, continuous, overbearing control. He might demand unreasonable financial accountability or a detailed accounting of her schedule, or he might even force his wife to perform all manner of perverted sexual acts, quoting Scripture to her about the need for wives "to be in subjection" to their husbands. I've heard many women say, "My husband always has to win; nothing else matters." As we have already learned, all of this is a mask for unresolved anger and personal inadequacy.

"Nobody Does Anything for Me"

There is the "Nobody does anything for me" controller. Guilt is an especially powerful tool for manipulation and control. Often those whose lives are in disarray have learned to transfer all responsibility for their failures to others, usually the members of their family. One woman who was finally able to break free of her mother's obsessive abuse of guilt said, "My mother is the East Coast distributor for guilt; in fact, she owns the franchise!"

I think of the student in Chicago who told his girlfriend, "If you break up with me, I will drown myself in Lake Michigan." He wanted to transfer responsibility for his suicide (if it were to occur) to her as punishment for breaking the relationship. That attitude, in itself, is proof of her good judgment in ending the friendship.

Guilt sometimes takes a manipulative twist. A mother, without her husband's consent, promises a child a new pair of shoes. Then she goes to her husband for the money and he says, "No, we can't afford it." She angrily responds, "Okay, if you are too stingy to do this, you be the one to tell our daughter that you won't buy her shoes. I want to make it clear that this is your fault, not mine!" Thus, the husband is manipulated into doing what she wanted.

Obsessive-Compulsive Controllers

Some people live with obsessive-compulsive controllers, who are "distinguished by repetitive, almost unstoppable thought patterns that lead to a powerful need to perform according to a rigid system of duties and obligations."[1] When they get a particular idea in mind, they cannot let it go until they have made every effort to act upon it. Because of their need to perform correctly, they often have shut down emotionally lest their emotions interfere with the need to follow through with their compulsive behavior. They tend to become angry and distraught when circumstances will not let them act out their repetitive behavior. Some wash their hands dozens of times a day, angry at dirt and germs, determined to control their health; others clean the house twice a day, sometimes in the middle of the night. Of course, they expect those around them to adopt their view of reality.

In summary, the controller is never satisfied, for every future event must continue to be controlled. Even if he manages to control everyone around him on any given day, the process begins again tomorrow. If nothing else, he will create a new crisis so that he will have something to control. Of course, controllers are never happy because something always has the potential of being out of control.

Controllers are also angered when someone, somewhere, gets by with something for which they deserve punishment. When a perceived injustice is against them, controllers become defensive, dig in their heels, and resort to every tactic available until the perpetrator "pays the last cent." If they think someone is being overpaid, especially if they suspect injustice, they are deeply bothered. They see the people around them, not as individuals to be loved as they are, but as potential rivals who need to be kept in line. They find it hard to rejoice over another's good fortune and hard to forgive.

Proper Control

When is control proper? Parents should control their children, if by that we mean teaching them right from wrong, loving them, and disciplining them for violations. Husbands should take control of their families, if by that we mean they become responsible for their welfare. We all should control the members of our body, so that we are not led into sin; indeed, the fruit of the Spirit is, among other things, "self-control." But, obviously, some forms of control are sinful and evil.

Manipulative, controlling parents have a tremendous authority over their children, so much so that it often continues after the parent has died. Many children today still make decisions based on what they think their parents would want them to do. Others react and do just the opposite, often to their detriment. This creates problems in new marriages and confusing parenting habits for the next generation. Thus, these grown children who have been sinned against react by sinning against others.

Children must come to the conclusion that their parents can be wrong. Yes, just because someone is your father or mother does not make them right in their decisions; nor is their perception of you always correct. Jesus came to set son against father and daughter against mother, affirming that sometimes He divides families (see Matt. 10:35).

And often children have to see the errors of their parents, forgive them, and distance themselves from their destructive influence.

There are some people with whom reconciliation is impossible because it must be done on their terms: One must admit to lying, though one has not lied; to deceit, though one has not been deceitful; to doing wrong where no wrong has been done. In short, the price of reconciliation is too high.

God often lets controllers become exasperated, until in desperation they surrender the circumstances and people around them to God and stop trying to control everything. They surrender control for two reasons: (1) control is God's responsibility, not ours, and (2) it does not work anyway! I speak to those of you who struggle with control issues: Have you actually changed the people you have tried to control?

Melody Beattie had a point when she wrote:

> We cannot change people. Any attempts to control them are a delusion as well as an illusion. People will either resist our efforts or redouble their efforts to prove we can't control them. They may temporarily adapt to our demands, but the moment we turn our backs they will return to their natural state. Furthermore, people will punish us for making them do something they don't want to do, or be something they don't want to be. No amount of control will effect a permanent or desirable change in another person. We can sometimes do things that increase the probability that people will want to change, but we can't even guarantee or control that.[2]

Here is a question that every controller should ponder: Why should you try to change others, when you cannot change yourself?

THE DISORDERED CONTROLLER

The term "borderline personality" refers to those who, when you meet them, appear to be normal, but the better you get to know them you discover them to be impulsive, to have a tendency to addictions, and to be wasteful in their spending habits. They are disordered, and because they dread being alone, they tend to be flighty, running from place to place and from person to person, trying to find security and significance. They will commit themselves to one course of action but soon switch to another. They grew up in homes without love and security, so they really do not know themselves well enough to know what they want in life and will often invest their lives in irrelevant matters.

The "Let me keep you off balance" controller fosters disorder. These people will disrupt every peaceful situation to mask their own insecurities. They want to control, not so much to hide evil as to hide their disordered personality. They fear being found out for who they are; reality is frightening. Because they are narcissistic, every event is interpreted in relationship to themselves. As we've learned, such people ask two questions: (1) How does this make *me* look? and (2) How does this make *me* feel? In other words, What is in it for *me*?

If the wife is a borderline, she will control her environment through unexpected mood shifts so that those in her vicinity are constantly off balance, not knowing what will happen next. She might be a hypochondriac, feigning endless symptoms of imaginary diseases. Or violent, irrational anger will keep the mood of the family unsettled, moving from incredible heights to lows, from hope that things will change to the despair of knowing that the patterns will be repeated.

The mate living with such a person refuses to comment on what he thinks or feels about anything because he is afraid of her reaction. He must walk on eggshells because he knows that whatever he says or does will be twisted and held against him. He can identify with the Psalmist: "They distort my words; All their thoughts are against me for evil" (Ps. 56:5 NASB). He will be blamed for what is wrong in the relationship even if it makes no sense; he will be told that his needs are unimportant in comparison to the never-ending needs of the narcissist.

If the husband is borderline, and his wife makes him hard-boiled eggs, he will want them scrambled that particular morning (and she should have known). If she makes them scrambled, he is angry because he wanted them fried. To use a football metaphor: The goalposts are always moved to ensure that the partner will be unable to kick the field goal. It is almost impossible to plan anything (such as social events) because of the inability to predict his moods—and what is worse, the wife begins to think that her husband's behavior is normal. She might begin to doubt her own sanity.

What makes it difficult is that these personalities alternate between being in a good mood and switching to an angry mood all within a few moments. Those who live with the borderline controlling personality often do not know which is real—is it the kind person who can, at times, be fun or the one who is irrationally angry, tense, and illogical? Is it the person who can be sociable when company is in the house or the one who can resort to chaos and disorder after the friends leave?

Borderline personalities categorize people as either good or bad; there is no ability for them to see the shades of evil and good. I knew a businessman who would become a close friend with an associate who could do no wrong, only to turn against him, damning him to hell because of minor differences. He would call people good if they lined up with his views; they were bad if they differed. Since it is virtually impossible for such a person to admit to his own faults, shifting blame, finding ingenious excuses, and becoming defensive become a lifestyle. The only way to be at peace with him is to agree with him.

Children growing up in a home in which there is mental illness will often adjust by adopting the insane perspective of the parent. At first they might see the errors, but eventually, if the parent's illness causes him to manipulate and control, the children will fall in line. Whoever the parent demonizes, the children demonize; whoever the parent honors, the children will honor. So convinced are the mentally ill that their view of reality is correct that they may cause their mate to doubt his/her sanity. But to maintain their illusionary world, the mentally ill will have to withdraw from all meaningful contact with others. They have lost the ability to test reality, and they are terrified of exposure.

THE EVIL CONTROLLER

Although the word *evil* can be variously defined, I am using it here to denote those people who are committed to the destruction of other people to protect themselves, to exalt themselves, and/or to vent their own anger. The evil person lies to benefit himself; he destroys to benefit himself; he schemes to benefit himself; he lives to benefit himself. He sits on the throne of his life as a god, exercising every bit of power he can to try to shape reality according to his fancy. He enjoys wielding the power of destruction, watching people squirm. And he will do anything to protect himself—his *sick* self. Meanwhile, he remains immune from blame or censure. Consider the words of M. Scott Peck:

> The words "image" and "appearance" and "outwardly" are crucial to understanding the morality of evil. While they seem to lack any motivation to *be* good, they intensely desire to appear good. Their "goodness" is all on the level of pretense. It is in effect, a lie. This is why they are "people of the lie."
>
> Actually, the lie is designed not so much to deceive others as to deceive themselves. They cannot or will not tolerate the pain of self-reproach. The decorum with which they lead their lives is maintained as a mirror in which they can see themselves reflected righteously. . . . It often happens, then, that the evil may be recognized by its very disguise. The lie can be perceived before the misdeed it is designed to hide—the cover-up before the fact. We see the smile that hides the hatred, the smooth and oily manner that masks the fury, the velvet glove that covers the fist. Because they are such experts at disguise, it is seldom possible to pinpoint the maliciousness of the evil. The disguise is unusually impenetrable.[3]

In a footnote, Peck says that since the primary motive of the evil one is the disguise, evil people are often found in church, an ideal place to conceal one's evil from one's self and others.[4] The evil person's greatest fear is that his subjects will no longer obey him, so he builds a protective shell around himself that will insulate him from the reality of the damage he is doing. This also serves to deaden his conscience, so that he can exercise his control without his emotions getting in the way. He will withdraw from anyone who does not see life through his set of glasses, that is, anyone he cannot control. No facts or evidence are ever allowed to stand as evidence of his own sinfulness. He is convinced he is blameless.

One controlling father would discipline his children in minor matters, using accusatory language, and if his daughter was reduced to tears he made light of it, asking why she could not take a joke. If he slapped her, he told her not to tell her mother because it would upset her. If she did tell, he would put the blame on the daughter: "You are the one who is causing me and your mother to fight," or "You made your mother cry all night." When she was ready to leave home, he tried to control where she would attend school, whom she would marry, and what she and her husband would do. When she tried to rebuff him, he would use guilt: "Just think of all I did for you! I paid for your college! We gave you a wonderful wedding. Do I deserve *this?*"

He treated his son with the same manipulative control. When he saw that he was losing control, he turned evil, trying to destroy the ministry of his own son and daughter-in-law, who by now had started an inner-city ministry. He discredited them and isolated them from the rest of his family with lies, innuendos, and accusations (as Satan the evil controller tries to divide friend from friend by accusations, questions, and innuendo). He told them that they were no longer welcome in his home then accused them of trying to keep his grandchildren from him. Like a drowning man reaching for a straw, this was his last gasp. Even though he was destroying those he professed to love, he disavowed personal responsibility for his actions. He thought of himself as an upright Christian who deserved to be respected and whose church ministry was crucial.

One man, who at one time aspired to missionary service, sought reasons to divorce his wife so he could be free to marry another woman with whom he was in love. In order to believe the myth of his own innocence, he concocted lies about his wife, making her out to be the one responsible for the breakup of his marriage.

He demonized her in the presence of their only child, destroying her reputation. Con man that he was, he manipulated bank accounts and cheated credit-card companies. With cunning intent he showed kindness, but only to twist the knife a bit further, trying to kill his wife one deception at a time. She lost every battle for the simple reason that he played by his own perverted rules, without a trace of conscience, without an ounce of feeling or decency. Remember, *the truly evil person does not see the world as it is; he sees only himself.*

Peck says that his experiences show that evil human beings are quite common and usually appear quite ordinary to the superficial observer.[5] They find sadistic delight in spooking people by invading their privacy, finding their unlisted phone numbers, stalking them, and leaving hints of their intentions. They want to keep their prey off balance by changing the rules of the relationship and promising one thing and doing another. They are murderers, not of the body, but of the spirit; not with a gun, but with evil twists and turns of behavior. If confronted, they will respond with cleverly crafted self-protection, excuses, denials, and more power plays. If they ever give an inch, it is to take a mile. Evil has an eye for weakness and exploits it.

Here in Chicago, a church member who unsuccessfully attempted to control the leadership of his church left with perhaps twenty followers to begin his own cult. He kept his followers in complete control: They could not buy groceries without his permission, he directed them on how they should use their finances, and women were subjected to repeated humiliation, using the Scriptures out of context. He would probe to find his followers' private sins so that he could keep them in a state of fear and intimidation. He also accused them of things they did not do, to maintain further control. Some in the group questioned their own sanity, believing that their leader could not possibly be wrong. He exempted himself from all criticism or challenge. Those who questioned his authority were told that they were falling under the judgment of God and were warned that their lives would come to ruin.

A terrified young woman came to our church and told us about an evil control freak who would lure young women with gifts, promises, and charming adoration until he had sex with them. Then the women were enslaved, subject to his every whim by abuse, intimidation, and meticulous control. This young woman's life was threatened and her spirit destroyed, and her will had become captive to this man's twisted beliefs. Though we urged her not to return to him, she defied us and went back, explaining that his "control was too powerful to resist." I've often wondered what happened to her.

CONTROL FREAKS, YOU, AND GOD

King Saul was a consummate control freak who crossed the line and became evil. He disobeyed God because he feared the Philistines and he feared the people (see 1 Sam. 12–15). This in itself should tell us something about his personality weakness. Yes, he was a coward; yes, he disobeyed, but all of us have sinned in this way. What made the potential evil in Saul erupt was when God told him that the kingdom would be taken away from him and given to another. The rise of David as a national hero terrified him, and he (Saul) lashed out, attempting to destroy someone who exposed his own weakness.

What are the characteristics of an evil controller?

Owners, Not Stewards

First, he thinks the kingdom is his and not God's. When Saul heard that God had chosen to give the kingdom to another, he should have accepted the verdict of the Lord; after all, God has the right to give the kingdom to whomever He wills (see 1 Sam. 15:26). But though Saul admitted he had sinned, he was determined to hang on to the kingdom until his knuckles turned white.

If there is one single reason why good people turn evil, it is because they fail to recognize God's ownership over their kingdom, their vocation, their resources, their abilities, and above all, their lives. Their insistence that they are owners and not stewards leads them to destroy others in order to protect what they perceive as theirs. They derive their sense of significance and value only through power, watching people squirm under their heavy hand. They are threatened by the realization that what they have is from God, who can give and take as He wills.

I've known pastors who have hung on to their "kingdom" despite the fact that their credibility had been destroyed and their time to leave had long since past. One minister would not resign though his anger had destroyed important relationships; another continued though his personal deceptions had come to light. Yes, there are times to stay and fight; but there are also times to leave when it is clear that the people of God are being torn asunder and the presence of the pastor is wounding the sheep rather than healing them. But some would rather destroy the kingdom to protect their own egos than entrust it into the hands of the One to whom it belongs.

Paranoia

Second, evil people fear those who might expose their weaknesses, and they become obsessed with jealousy and rage at the thought that someone might upstage them.

When the women of Israel credited Saul with having killed thousands, but David "tens of thousands," we read, "Saul was very angry; this refrain galled him. 'They have credited David with tens of thousands,' he thought, 'but me with only thousands. What more can he get but the kingdom?' And from that time on Saul kept a jealous eye on David" (1 Sam. 18:7–9). Little wonder we read that an evil spirit entered Saul and he took a spear and hurled it at David, trying to kill him.

The controller becomes obsessed, willing to resort to violence if he sees his control slipping away. He suffers from paranoia, believing that the whole world is out to get him. Actually, in Saul's case he had nothing to fear, for David most assuredly was not going to take the kingdom from him. But to the controller, everyone he cannot control is his enemy.

Slander

Third, a controller always tries to drive a wedge between people to isolate those whose opinions and actions he cannot control. Saul tried to drive a wedge between Jonathan and David, asking his son to kill his best friend (see 1 Sam. 19:1)! A controller will destroy the reputation of those around him and stir up strife between friends. Under the guise of trying to be helpful, he will privately criticize the one person to the other; he will appeal to the ego of the person he is trying to control as he discredits the person's friends. He will slander anyone who can bring an accusation against him, hoping to destroy the person's reputation so that when the accusation comes, he can dismiss it. In other words, the controller wants to make sure that all potential "enemies" are discredited before they can even fight.

When Jonathan refused to kill David, he received a tongue-lashing from his father. Saul called him "the son of a perverse and rebellious woman" (1 Sam. 20:30), berating him for bringing shame to the family. Here is the skillful art of projection: In speaking of his son, he was actually speaking of himself; for it is he, Saul, who was perverse and brought shame upon the family. *But the evil person sees his own sins as those of others.*

You might wonder whether Saul had any compassion for David. Early on in the relationship he professed love for David. But as time passed, his conscience was hardened. When a man gives himself to destroy others, he becomes emotionally numb, incapable of empathy. He actually disengages his emotions, so that he has no feeling for those he is hurting. His natural bent of caring is neutralized through rationalization and anger. Emotionally he is, as the saying goes, "zoned out."

Does not the father who abuses his son have sympathy for him as the child cries for mercy? The answer is no, he does not. The truly narcissistic, abusive personality is obsessed with only one thing: that his authority (control) be exercised. Control is his lifeblood; it is in the marrow of his bones; it is his one satisfaction, his one opportunity to show to himself (if not to others) that he really is someone after all. His anger at perceived injustices must be appeased. In his perverted thinking, abusing others is his only way of making this crooked world straight.

Manipulation

Fourth, Saul was a cunning manipulator, using kindness to kill. Since he was unable to kill David himself, he set up a trap so that the Philistines would do it for him. Saul appeared so magnanimous, so kind, that he was willing to honor David by giving his daughter Merab to him. Of course there was a catch: He hoped the act would provoke the wrath of the enemy and that the Philistines would kill David for him (see 1 Sam. 18:17, 30). Like Judas, Saul could make treachery look like loyalty.

Saul's false humility kept David off balance, for there were times when Saul could be charming and appear to be very accommodating. Five times he promised to mend his ways, saying that he was "repenting." No doubt this gave David hope, thinking that the king's attitude was changing for the better, perhaps permanently. Just as a control freak might repent and offer hope of reform, so Saul sent mixed signals. But eventually he would change his mind about having changed his mind.

No Rules

Finally, Saul refused to live by the rules he made for others. We read, "Saul had expelled the mediums and spiritists from the land" (1 Sam. 28:3). Yet, interestingly, four verses later we read that when the Philistine army came, Saul asked that the medium be found, so that he could receive her counsel. He disguised himself and went to the witch at

Endor, so that she might contact Samuel, who had just died, for him. He played by the rule of the "Grand Exception."

The controller is incapable of judging himself by the same standard he uses to judge others. What he does is right, by definition. This is why reasoning with an extreme control freak is utterly hopeless, for he does not hear the message. His raging desire for control meets a warped personal need and appears to be insatiable. All of reality is interpreted through his lens—a bent lens to be sure, but a lens nonetheless. He exercises his godhood, protecting his only source of personal identity.

What lessons should we draw from this story? Keep in mind that we all are born as control freaks. We want to be recognized, protected, nourished, and remembered. We must be willing to see the sins in our own lives before we react to the lives of others.

What did David learn during those ten years when Saul hunted him? Why does God allow evil controllers to go on exercising their powers? Why does He give power to those who don't deserve it? We've all known those who were excellent leaders, excellent communicators, and excellent spear-throwers, just like Saul.

Used by God

In his provocative book *A Tale of Three Kings,* Gene Edwards answers the question why God sometimes gives evil people power. "The answer is both simple and shocking. He sometimes gives unworthy vessels a greater portion of power so that it might eventually be revealed for all to see the true state of internal nakedness within that man."[6] He wants to show raw human nature, in all of its narcissistic, self-indulgent sinfulness. He wants to keep proving that human nature, apart from the intervention of common grace and saving grace, is ugly.

Speaking of us, Edwards writes, "Saul is in your bloodstream . . . in the marrow of your bones. He makes up the very flesh and muscle of your heart. He is mixed into your soul. He inhabits the nuclei of your atoms. King Saul is one with you."[7] When we look at Saul we are looking at ourselves. If our wills have never been brought into submission to God, if we do not have a secure identity apart from our performance, then any one of us could become a control freak of the worst sort. Controllers remind us of the desperate need for the intervention of God's undeserved grace.

God uses controllers for His own purposes, sometimes to refine those who have to put up with them! God used King Saul to take the Saul out of David's heart. Gene Edwards suggests that if David had not had a Saul who pursued him, he would have ended up as "Saul number II." Some of the most beautiful psalms were written when David was fleeing from Saul, needing to depend solely on the Lord for protection and comfort. Think of what we would have missed if Saul had never lived! (Read Psalms 34 and 59, for example.)

Free from Control

David teaches us that it is proper to try to get free from the controller's grip whenever possible. When Saul hurled spears at him, he fled. He did not stay in the vicinity, trying to be a martyr. If God wanted David to be murdered, that could have been arranged, but He was not about to make it easy for Saul to accomplish that.

If you are married to a controller, assure him that you want to help him "come to the light." Remember, he is afraid of exposure, afraid that he will be revealed as the empty, angry person he is. You yourself must approach the situation with a great deal of soul-searching to make sure that you are not contributing to the power struggle. Tell him that he can admit his anger, his guilt, and his sense of injustice and still be accepted. Don't dig in your heels, but try to see life from your spouse's point of view. If there is persistent abuse, *get help*.

Controllers need to know that Jesus can free them from the fear that makes them think that everyone who does not agree with them is their enemy. If we are children of God, we don't have to win all the time. The Holy Spirit can penetrate our carefully constructed radar system and show us that when we stop denying our sinfulness, healing can happen.

David also exercised restraint. To his everlasting credit, he did not wrench the spear out of the wall and throw it back. When you live with a spear-thrower, do not throw spears back. There is little use trying to argue with a control freak, throwing spear for spear, verbal attack for verbal attack. Our natural inclination is to try to justify ourselves and repay evil for evil, but the control freak always wins. Because remember, *a control freak is not interested in finding the truth, but only in proclaiming his version of it.*

David fought to distinguish between his perception of reality and Saul's insanity. In fact, David did actually "lose it" and lapsed into a mental imbalance. He himself feigned insanity and ended up joining the army of the Philistines to fight against his own people (see 1 Sam. 28)! Those who are stalked by a control freak must maintain their equilibrium, not just in their relationship with God, but also by keeping in touch with other people. We've said many times that the mentally deranged can make the mentally stable begin to question their own sanity. Just as the slave who said that the blows fell on his back but not on his soul, so those who are ill treated must not retaliate, but leave vengeance to God.

Wait on God

David waited on God. There is no doubt that God called David to live in pain. We shy away from that, of course, but it is in our pain that God refines us. And for some, that pain is to have to live with someone who is self-absorbed, emotionally disconnected, and uncaring.

"This poor man called, and the LORD heard him; he saved him out of all his troubles. The angel of the LORD encamps around those who fear him, and he delivers them" (Ps. 34:6–7). David learned something while waiting on God: He learned that he was in God's hands, not the hands of Saul, nor the hands of fate. I agree with the person who said, "Your friends can only take you to your potential; only your enemies can take you beyond it."

God can do what we cannot. We are often baffled by how long He allows the wicked to continue, but yet we have the promise: "Do not fret because of evil men or be envious of those who do wrong; for like the grass they will soon wither, like green plants they will soon die away" (Ps. 37:1–2). I am reminded of a two-year-old child in a stroller, angrily turning his little steering wheel to the right but going to the left, nonetheless. His direction was not determined by him, but by his mother; his steering wheel was not connected to anything that mattered.

Just so the wicked: They have the illusion of control, but their fate is in God's hands. How quickly their world can disintegrate; how quickly their lives can be brought to an end. While they do their evil deeds, we believe that God takes up the cause of the oppressed. I've just spoken to a woman whose husband has become evil in vile and rebellious ways, turning their children against her. She must watch as the children she loves are being destroyed morally and spiritually. Her friends have prayed and fasted, but there has been no answer or solution to the problem. We cry and say, "How long, O Lord?"

We are comforted with the thought that those who would play God's role will eventually be judged by Him. "Do not take revenge, my friends, but leave room for God's wrath, for it is written: 'It is mine to avenge; I will repay,' says the Lord" (Rom. 12:19).

OUR BEST EXAMPLE

Here is a final word for both the controllers and the controlled.

Jesus had the power to control all the events of His life, yet He exercised none of it. When a crowd gathered to arrest Him, He made an astounding statement: "This hour and the power of darkness are yours" (Luke 22:53 NASB). In effect He said, "Today you win; today you get to control the outcome of events. Go ahead, nail Me to the Cross."

These evil controllers went ahead with their diabolical deed, and as a result Christ purchased our redemption. The men were responsible, yes; but God would use these control freaks to accomplish His own purposes. Jesus teaches us this: *Because I believe My Father is in control, I don't have to be.*

Back in 1907, Adelaide Pollard was in a prayer meeting where someone prayed, "Lord, just have your way with us." The phrase stuck in her mind and later she wrote a poem that has been set to music:

> Have Thine own way, Lord!
> Have Thine own way!
> Thou art the potter; I am the clay.
> Mold me and make me after thy will,
> While I am waiting, yielded and still.

Yes, if God is in charge, we don't have to be.

A Promise to Ponder

Humble yourselves, therefore under God's mighty hand,
that he may lift you up in due time.
Cast all your anxiety on him because he cares for you.

—1 Pet. 5:6–7

CHAPTER 10
THE HEALING POWER OF THE LIGHT

The wife of a Christian businessman suspected her husband was having an affair with a woman he knew from work. She also knew that her husband was not one to admit to any wrongdoing; in their fifteen years of marriage she had seldom, if ever, heard him say, "I'm sorry, I was wrong." He always had to win.

Knowing that he was both secretive and protective of his own reputation, she set up a series of circumstances to confront him and give him the opportunity to tell the truth. First, she voiced her own suspicions, but he denied the accusations, saying that she was too paranoid and that he felt slighted that she didn't trust him. A few days later she confronted him with a church member present who had seen her husband with the woman in the downtown area. Again the husband denied any wrongdoing and gave a plausible explanation as to why he was with the lady. But more evidence was in the offing.

Next, the woman had her husband meet the ex-husband of the woman with whom she believed he was having the affair. The ex-husband said that earlier when he picked up his children, he saw the man in the apartment, partly dressed. But the presumed adulterer just stared the ex-husband down, calling him a liar. Finally, the man's wife showed him videotapes taken by a private investigator.

Knowing he was trapped, the man responded, "Okay, so I am having an affair. So what's the big deal?" The violation of his marriage vows and the fact that immorality grieves God evidently did not grip his mind. This transgression was a small sin, not a big one.

When caught in a sin, our first inclination is to deny it; when that becomes impossible, our next move is to minimize it. There are some people whose repentance comes too easily; they confess their sins to be sure, but there is no heartfelt recognition of wrong. Those whom they have sinned against feel deep pain in their hearts, but the offender is satisfied with a cursory admission of wrongdoing. Understandably, this man's wife was not quick to reconcile because she knew that, as Larry Crab says, *where sin is taken superficially, it is dealt with superficially.*

On one level it is true to say that our past can be put behind us through confession. But if we have minimized our transgressions, if we do not feel the pain of those we have wronged, if we are too quick to pronounce ourselves cured, if we chide those around us for not quickly forgetting what we've done, our repentance might be all too superficial. Recall in the previous chapter we learned that King Saul repented five times but always returned to his evil behavior. Repentance, if it is to be effective, must be understood. More of that later.

Why do we find it so difficult to come to the light? Why does truth sometimes have to be pulled out of us like a sliver pulled from our finger with tweezers? There are many reasons: First, we might be enjoying our sin, unwilling to part with it; second, we don't want to be shamed or, to put it differently, we do not want our reputation to be sullied. Left to ourselves, we hate the light of truth; we hate it at any cost. As we learned back in chapter 1, the self that we present to others in our social relationships is often quite different from the self that actually exists.

Not all those who walk in darkness are dishonest; sometimes they are just concealing their memories to hide their pain. A woman whom we shall call Rachel grew up in what appeared to be a fine Christian home. Though her father was well liked as a Sunday school teacher, he would sexually abuse his daughter at home then make her lie in cold water, warning that if she ever told, she would pay the consequences. One time he tied her up in the outdoor toilet facility as punishment for a petty disobedience. His harshness was always mingled with an apparent tenderness about church and the Bible. He would ask his daughter to sing hymns for him and generously reward her with gifts and money. Of course, though he would have denied it, this was in effect hush money, intended to buy her silence. Yet, he would come into her bedroom at night and expect her to engage in various forms of sex.

What hurt Rachel even more was that her mother appeared to be oblivious to what was going on. Her father intimidated her mother with threats and brief fits of temper. If her mother knew about her husband's evil ways, she kept silent, possibly out of fear of retaliation. When at the age of fourteen Rachel had an argument with her father, refusing his demands for sexual favors, he pushed her down the stairs and told her to leave home. She chose not to leave, and he did not bring up the subject again. But three years later Rachel did leave home at age seventeen to live with her high-school boyfriend.

Five years and several boyfriends later, she married, but the relationship soon soured. Rachel could not relate to her husband sexually and found herself depressed and angry. She had determined that no one would ever know of her past, especially of her relationship with her father. She treated her husband with contempt, and her angry, unfounded accusations against him escalated. *Having been sinned against by her father, she sinned against her husband.*

Rachel resisted counseling. Why should she, the victim of evil, have to do the revealing, the forgiving, and the admitting of her own sins? But when divorce was imminent, she finally agreed to see a counselor. There, in the presence of a caring woman, Rachel finally told her story, and for the first time the secret she had so carefully guarded was brought to the light.

The rest of the story is a happy one. Though many women never do recover from sexual abuse, Rachel has made a great deal of progress. Now that her husband understands the reasons for her emotional outbursts and she has been able to face the pain of her past, the truth is setting her free. She had to learn, as all of us must, that unless we are willing to bring the dark part of ourselves to the light, the darkness will continue.

The man who committed adultery had to come to the light in order to be cleansed from the deceit of immorality; Rachel had to come to the light to deal with the evil deeds of her father and her own subsequent sin against her husband. Though their stories are different, they have this in common: Only the light could heal them.

The premise of this chapter is that, although the truth hurts, lies hurt even more. Therefore we must leave the darkness and come into the light, where there are forgiveness, reconciliation, and healing. Only truth in the presence of God sets us free.

Keep in mind that there are some people who will never come to the light. They are so content with themselves, so satisfied with their self-confidence, so convinced of their personal righteousness, that they see no need for change. They confuse darkness with light, often with a settled assurance that makes those who know them gasp. "But the way of the wicked is like deep darkness; they do not know what makes them stumble" (Prov. 4:19). Since they are not sure where they are going, any path will get them there.

WALKING IN THE LIGHT

A businessman called his pastor, sobbing on the phone, asking him to come over immediately. When the pastor arrived at the man's office, the man was slumped over his desk, sobbing so violently he was unable to speak. The pastor thought for certain that the man's wife had died, or perhaps a child. But when the man was able to gain his composure, he said, "God has just shown me my heart, and it was as if I were looking into the pit of hell."

What sin had this man committed? Murder? Adultery? Grand theft? No; he had, however, falsified some expense accounts while doing business for his company. The total amount was quite small, perhaps a few hundred dollars over a period of years. Most businessmen would think nothing of it; such minor infractions are done all the time. This man's sin was small in comparison to that of others. Small, that is, *until he saw God!*

What a difference light makes! In the presence of the Almighty, all rationalizations fade into oblivion. No sin is minor; every infraction is a "big deal." Only when we compare ourselves with ourselves do we think that our sins are not too serious. But in the presence of God, we see ourselves as we are, not how we wish we were. One difference between superficial repentance and genuine repentance is that the first is based on being discovered by men; the second is based on being "discovered" by God.

Back on the farm we had a musty basement that we dared not enter without a flashlight. The moment the light shone, the bugs would scurry between the cracks and under the debris. These vermin could roam freely only in the darkness and were dissipated in the light. Just so sin cannot lodge in our hearts if we are "walking in the light." As a general rule, we can say that the greater our sin, the more resistant we are to the light. Martin Buber described this when he said, "The uncanny game of hide and seek in the obscurity of the soul is one in which the single human soul, evades itself, avoids itself and hides from itself."[1]

Whatever pain walking in the light brings, the healing it brings is worth the price. For in the light my false self is exposed, I admit who I am, and I experience God's indescribable grace. Either I cry to God for mercy for my sin, or I hate the light that showed it to me.

Light Reveals Who We Are

Walk away from a street lamp and you will notice your shadow becoming longer, so long in fact that it will eventually fade into the distance. But as you come under the light, there will be no shadow at all. Mark it well: If we want to take a true measure of ourselves, we must come into the light of God's presence through His Word. There I will not measure myself by my achievements or by the opinion of those around me, not even by my opinion of myself. There I am who I am in the presence of the One who knows me and loves me. "For you were once darkness, but now you are light in the Lord. Live as children of light" (Eph. 5:8).

Let's remind ourselves that those who have seen a revelation of God have always been humbled, devastated by the scope of their sinfulness. Job was upset with the Almighty, in effect blaming Him for his seemingly unjust calamities. But when he saw God, he replied, "I am unworthy—how can I reply to you? I put my hand over my mouth. I spoke once, but I have no answer—twice, but I will say no more. . . . My ears had heard of you but now my eyes have seen you. Therefore I despise myself and repent in dust and ashes" (Job 40:4–5; 42:5–6). Darkness is what I think about myself; light is what God thinks about me.

Isaiah had a vision of God and replied, "Woe to me! . . . I am ruined! For I am a man of unclean lips, and I live among a people of unclean lips, and my eyes have seen the King, the LORD Almighty" (Isa. 6:5). Peter, recognizing Jesus to be the Christ, said, "Go away from me, Lord; I am a sinful man!" (Luke 5:8). We cannot approach the light without being keenly aware that darkness resides in our hearts.

Thankfully, whenever God reveals our darkness, it is so that we might be brought to the light. There is a fable about a deep underground cave that was challenged to come to the surface to see the light. But the cave replied that there was no such thing as light, only darkness. But, one day, the cave chose to come to the surface, and much to its surprise it enjoyed the light. Then the cave challenged the sun to come underground to experience darkness, and the sun took up the challenge. But when the sun went underground to visit the cave, it asked, "Where is the darkness? I cannot find it!" When God comes, He both reveals the darkness and dissipates it.

If I continue to deny the dark side of me—the part that seems so unlovable—then I cannot walk in the light. For light cannot shine when there is dishonesty. "If we claim to have fellowship with him yet walk in darkness, we lie and do not live by the truth" (1 John 1:6). And if I confess the darkness that I know about, God will graciously forgive the darkness of which I am not aware. That, I think, is what John meant when he wrote, "If we walk in the light, as he is in the light, we have fellowship with one another, and the blood of Jesus, his Son, purifies us from all sin" (1 John 1:7).

"It is the nature of the false self," wrote James Masterson, "to save us from knowing the truth about our real selves, from penetrating the deeper causes of our unhappiness, from seeing ourselves as we really are—vulnerable, afraid, terrified, and unable to let our real selves emerge."[2] Keep in mind that a surgeon cuts, but only in order to heal. The pain brings gain, the wounds turn into scars, and the false turns into reality. Light not only *reveals,* but also *heals.*

Light Reveals Our Path

When we come to the light, we find a host of fellow travelers who are also lovers of light. We as believers have "fellowship one with another" and can lock arms for every step of the journey. On the farm, a lantern showed us only the next step, but after we took it, we could see the next step. And so it was we walked all the way to the barn in the cold, dark night. "Your word is a lamp to my feet and a light for my path" (Ps. 119:105). Only in the light is our conscience brought to peace and our lives ordered by the Lord. Omar Bradley said, "We need to learn to set our course by the stars, not by the lights of every passing ship." Only the light will take us where we need to go. And only faith can entrust the consequences to God.

A woman whom we shall call Marie had to confess to her husband that she was involved in an affair with a man who was a friend of her husband. She had no idea what the impact of this revelation would mean for her marriage, particularly because she was pregnant and not sure whether the child was her husband's. To come to the light was not only painful and, for that matter, shameful, but it was also devastating for her husband. For weeks she struggled, thinking that the pain of concealment might be better than the pain of honest revelation. But how could she live with herself, and with her God, while her conscience was destroying her peace of mind? She would have to come to the light and leave the consequences to God.

Yes, the consequences were torturous. But, in this case, her husband was willing to forgive, to restore, and to commit himself to openness in their relationship (turns out that he had a few things to confess as well, such as pornography and an emotional attachment to another woman). Their marriage survived the storm, and the good news is that a paternity test revealed that the husband was the father. My point: We must come to the light even if we do not know what the consequences will be. You've heard the old saying "It is never too late to do what is right."

Only light can show the way.

Light Reveals Our Destination

Interestingly, those who walk in darkness end in "outer darkness"; those who walk in light will spend eternity "walking with God in light." We read, "The city does not need the sun or the moon to shine on it, for the glory of God gives it light, and the Lamb is its lamp" (Rev. 21:23). The way we live on this side of the grave determines how we shall live when we have passed through the parted curtain. "The path of the righteous is like the first gleam of dawn, shining ever brighter till the full light of day" (Prov. 4:18).

When a miser was dying, he asked his daughter to blow out the one candle in his room. "But, Daddy . . . don't you suppose . . ." Her words trailed off and he said, "I don't need light to die." He lived in darkness, died in darkness, and would spend eternity in darkness. How different is the eternal fate of those who come to the light to receive God's forgiveness and find the grace He promised. "For God, who said, 'Let light shine out of darkness,' made his light shine in our hearts to give us the light of the knowledge of the glory of God in the face of Christ" (2 Cor. 4:6).

THE COST OF COMING TO THE LIGHT

Why don't we come to the light? We believe that the pain we will experience will be much greater than the benefit we will receive. Unfortunately, the frowns of our friends often mean more to us than the smile of God. We must overcome our natural inclination to hide our shame and come to the light, no matter the cost.

The false self, that part of me that denies my greed and self-centeredness can never be healed without exposure. That part of me that draws significance from achievements and the adulation of others, that part of me that withdraws from those who are a threat to me, that part of me that judges others for sins of which I am guilty—it is the part of me that must be brought to the light. When the false self is exposed, and we know we are radically loved by God, we are truly free. Brennan Manning quotes Barbara Finand: "Wholeness is brokenness owned and thereby healed."[3]

For some, the cost of coming to the light is monetary. A Christian contractor had cheated his clients by putting inferior materials into the houses he built. In short, he promised them one quality of boards, insulation, and the like but gave them another. When he tried to be honest in the presence of God, he could not escape his dishonesty and thievery. No matter how he rationalized it, no matter how often he confessed his sin to God, he knew that he could never be at peace as long as restitution was within his power. When he finally did what he knew he should, he went to the bank and borrowed money to repay his customers. "Fellowship with God has cost me thousands of dollars," he told me, "but it is worth every penny."

For some, the cost is one of shameful revelation. A man who was being considered for the position of deacon in a church initially said yes, he would accept, but then he backed out. His first inclination was to simply say he was too busy for the job, but he knew that wasn't true. He would be "adding sin to sin," as the Scripture warns. So he confessed the truth, that he had fallen into the habit of visiting prostitutes, and try as he might, he could not shake the habit. Yes, he also owed an explanation to his wife, since he had lied to her about his whereabouts from time to time. Since he was so well thought of, the confession was excruciating because he thought he could never be loved and respected again. But when God compels us to come to the light, any price is worth it because He is our most precious possession.

King David committed adultery and he tried to hide it; he murdered a man as part of the cover-up. As usually happens, the cover-up came unraveled as lies were told to cover lies. The embarrassment of what he had done drove him to silence; though he could manage lying to men, he could not bear the thought that these lies were told in the presence of the God he loved. The contrast between living a lie and being in fellowship with God is detailed for us in Psalm 32.

Of course, some people think that the cost of fellowship with God is just too much to pay. A Christian man who falsified an application form for workmen's compensation would not come to the light, though his pastor told him he should. He sustained an injury on a vacation that he reported as having happened on his job. He now receives a monthly paycheck and will do so till he dies. Let me quote his words: "Do you think that I am going to confess to the compensation board? I'd go to jail for it. Sorry, but I want to keep things the way they are." He does not realize it would be better to walk in the light in jail than to walk in darkness as a "free" man, as the next story illustrates.

For one man, "coming to the light" cost a lifetime jail sentence. On the morning of December 21, 1975, fourteen-year-old John Claypool shot and killed his neighbor and his neighbor's wife for no reason other than to feel what it was like to see someone die. Though the police questioned him and he was the prime suspect, he was let go for lack of direct evidence. He writes, "Yet this awful deed lived on in my mind as a deep, dark secret. I told no one, and I planned to take my secret to the grave."

Eventually he married and had two children, but then his wife left him. God brought some Christians into his life and he yearned for the peace they had. "This yearning for peace with God was driven by the constant weight that I felt in my soul from my sin." He purchased a Bible and realized that Jesus could save him from his sins. He was converted. Now his heart pounded in fear as the Holy Spirit seemed to say to him, "My child, you must obey Me by confessing your crime or you will never know My full blessing on your life."

He told a woman he was dating at the time about his dark secret and she broke up with him. Finally, on November 27, 1995, with the help of his pastor and an attorney, he surrendered to the authorities. Great fear gripped him as by now he was in the spotlight of the public media.

Afterward, John Claypool said,

> Yet God was faithful to His promise to uphold me. At the moment of truth, though I was now a prisoner of the law, I was set free before God for the first time in my life. I cannot describe the feeling of that burden completely lifted—the Lord now held His once-disobedient child in His loving arms; and true to His promise, He did not let me fall! A wonderful peace came over my soul, such as I had never known before.
>
> I am now confined in a maximum-security prison, serving time for second-degree murder. But I am more free and more at peace than at any other time in my life.[4]

Was coming to the light worth it? Yes. Is it worth a clear conscience? Perhaps yes, perhaps no. But what we will not do for a clear conscience we should be willing to do for the God we love. Pleasing Him is always worth it, no matter the cost. Sitting in jail, John Claypool is being healed by the light.

TRANSFORMING LESSONS

Let's remember these lessons as we think about coming to the light.

1. *What we hide hurts.* There is some truth to the statement that you are only as sick as your darkest secrets. That is true for the person who

has sinned, as well as for the person who has been sinned against. Those who have been the victims of injustice and now are vindictive toward others also must come to the light.

Of course, "coming to the light" means different things for different people. For all of us it means honesty before God, humbly facing our thoughts, desires, and actions, no matter how shameful they might be. For some, it means the need to be reconciled to others or the need to be counseled and affirmed by those they trust. Remember, the purpose is not simply to expose the darkness, but to enjoy the light.

2. *What we hide grieves God.* During times of revival, the conviction of the Holy Spirit is so powerful that people see small sins as being large ones. What is more, their desire to please God is greater than their desire to hide their sins. Our relationship with God is nonnegotiable; it cannot be reasoned away. "You have set our iniquities before you, our secret sins in the light of your presence" (Ps. 90:8).

Most people think it is unnecessary for God to search them, for they already know that they are right and the other person is wrong. They don't understand the radical dimension of what honesty with God might reveal. Our love for God is our greatest motivation to come to the light, and when we have Him, we are loved, accepted, and secure. But we cannot have intimacy with Him unless we are our true selves in His presence.

3. *Light and darkness cannot coexist.* When we see light, we must either move toward it or move back into the darkness. And if we retreat into the darkness, our hearts will become a little harder and we will become more comfortable with the darkness. If you ask why some people become evil (as described in the previous chapter), it is because when faced with the choice of coming to the light or turning away into deeper darkness, they choose the darkness. We should not be surprised that among the truly evil are some who at one time appeared to walk in the light. For the greater the light we reject, the greater the darkness we must accept.

4. *The question is not whether we have come to the light, but whether*

we are now walking in it. Sometimes when someone falls into sin—immorality, for example—we ask: Did he repent? But actually the better question is: Is he repenting? The person who has come to the light in the past might be walking in darkness today. Coming to the light is only the first step in the journey of life. In fact, I should be walking in greater light today than I did yesterday. Life is a journey and only becomes a destination at death.

Can a Christian who has walked in the light return to darkness? Yes. As we already learned, "If *we* claim to have fellowship with him yet walk in the darkness, *we* lie and do not live by the truth" (1 John 1:6; emphasis added). However, it is also true that those who continue to live in darkness will incur the discipline of God.

GETTING FOUND

Robert Fulghum, in *All I Really Needed to Know I Learned in Kindergarten,* tells how in October when he was a child, he and his friends would play hide-and-seek under the leaves. There was always one kid who hid so well that nobody could find him. Eventually, the others gave up on him. When he finally showed up, they would explain that there was hiding and there was finding, and he was not to hide in such a way that he could not be found.

Fulghum continues:

> As I write this, the neighborhood game goes on, and there is a kid under a pile of leaves in the yard just under my window. He has been there a long time now, and everybody else is found and they are about to give up on him over at the base. I considered going out to the base and telling them where he is hiding. And I thought about setting the leaves on fire to drive him out. Finally, I just yelled, "GET FOUND, KID!" out the window. And it scared him so bad he probably . . . started crying and ran home to tell his mother. It is real hard to know how to be helpful sometimes.[5]

Some who are reading this chapter are playing hide-and-seek grown-up style. We want to hide so well we will never be found. We all have hidden under stacks of leaves so skillfully arranged that no one can see us. At first we congratulate ourselves, for there is a sense of security in knowing that no one can find us. But eventually God turns our cubbyhole into a private hell. Eventually, we want to be found out, no matter the cost.

"Search me, O God, and know my heart; test me and know my anxious thoughts. See if there is any offensive way in me, and lead me in the way everlasting" (Ps. 139:23–24). So I shout to you under your pile of rationalizations, under your pile of bitterness, under your pile of deception: GET FOUND!

A Promise to Ponder

Search me, O God, and know my heart;

test me and know my anxious thoughts.

See if there is any offensive way in me,

and lead me in the way everlasting.

—Ps. 139:23–24

CHAPTER 11
A BAD MAN MADE GOOD

In the book *Dr. Jekyll and Mr. Hyde*, Robert Louis Stevenson wants us to grapple with the deceptions and potential evil within our hearts. The thesis of the book is that man is not really one, but two. One part of man is noble, cultured, and good; another part is filled with primitive impulses and animal desires. Since these two forces are chained together, man is locked in a struggle. The good man (the intellect) represses the evil man (the animal desires). The good is stifled by the evil; the evil is in remorse because it is constantly restricted by the good.

The story is an experiment of what would happen if the two were separated: The good would be free to become better, filled with acts of kindness and noble ambition; the evil would become thoroughly evil because the corruption and deception could develop without restriction. In the movie version of the story, the man drinks a potion and thus moves back and forth between the good Dr. Jekyll and the evil Mr. Hyde. Dr. Jekyll wins the heart of a young woman, but after drinking a potion, he terrorizes her. The transformation is so complete, the butler in the house thinks that two men are actually living in the home. The story is true to experience: Many a woman will tell you that she walked down the aisle of the church thinking she was marrying the kind Dr. Jekyll, only to wake up on her honeymoon to discover that she was in bed with Mr. Hyde.

Of course we are only one person, but we all have felt the conflict between what we know is right and what our desires want to do. Peter warned, "Dear friends, I urge you, as aliens and strangers in the world, to abstain from sinful desires, which war against your soul" (1 Peter 2:11). If we follow our desires wherever they lead, our lives can spin out of control very quickly. Read the words of Oscar Wilde, who wrote about the depth of his own depravity when he chose to follow his animal instincts:

> The gods have given me almost everything. But I let myself be lured into long spells of senseless and sensual ease. . . . Tired of being on the heights, I deliberately went to the depths in search for a new sensation. What the paradox was to me in the sphere of thought, perversity became to me in the sphere of passion. . . . I took pleasure where it pleased me, and passed on. I forgot that little actions of the common day make or unmake character, and that therefore what one has done in the secret chamber, one has some day to cry aloud from the housestop. I was no longer the captain of my soul and did not know it. I allowed pleasure to dominate me. I ended in horrible disgrace.[1]

Could this be my story or your story? Yes, if we simply set foot on the same path. On the one hand we are created in the image of God with a moral consciousness and endless capacities for development and creativity; on the other hand our nature has been corrupted by sin and therefore is capable of evil. As already emphasized, even Christians with a new nature can fall into deep sin and commit crimes. But there is a difference: Those who have come to trust Christ have the resources to live differently, and if they do not, they will be disciplined by our Father in heaven. And if they are not so disciplined, they disprove the genuineness of their faith (see Heb. 12:8).

GOOD PEOPLE, BAD THINGS

In these chapters we have tried to give a candid appraisal of the human heart in order to see our rationalizations and penchant for self-deception. So, having come this far, we ask once again: Why do good people do bad things? Actually, the question itself is suspect.

Strictly speaking, not one of us is good. When a young man came to Jesus and said to Him, "Good teacher . . . what must I do to inherit eternal life?" Jesus replied, "Why do you call me good? No one is good—except God alone" (Mark 10:17–18). Quite obviously, Jesus wanted him to realize that He (Jesus) was actually good and therefore should be called God. But the point stands: No one is good but God.

Most people have not come to grips with the potential for evil that exists in all our hearts. Yes, there are important differences between people. Some are kind and caring; others are cruel and selfish. But if we stop comparing ourselves with one another and compare ourselves with God, who is the absolute standard of goodness, the differences between us are less obvious: No one is good but God. In medical terminology, we are born with a preexisting condition. Sin has entered the human race, and we are badly affected.

Second, we've learned that we are tempted to submit to our untamed desires, not to reason or to the commands of Scripture. We are led astray because we want to be, so we want to fashion a God who agrees with us and approves of our deepest cravings. A series of small steps taken in the wrong direction eventually leads to a severe spiritual and moral blowout. We tell ourselves that we can control the consequences of actions that we intuitively know are wrong.

Many years ago some friends invited my wife and me to their new home in northern Wisconsin in the dead of winter. One evening they decided to take us out for dinner to a secluded restaurant about ten miles away. About five miles down the road they realized that we were on the wrong country road. The car made deep fresh ruts in the snow; the farther we went, the more bleak our surroundings and the deeper the snow. We were headed for no man's land. We tried to turn around at a crossroad but were stuck there for about an hour and half, with temperatures hovering around zero. Thanks to a shovel and some ingenuity, we turned the vehicle around and headed for home.

We learned several lessons that night. First, a wrong turn can cause us to lose time that can never be regained. We never did get to eat at that restaurant; in fact, my wife and I have never been there to this day. Just so, some people lose years of their lives because of personal sin, whether addictions, broken marriages, or misplaced priorities.

A second lesson is that our failures can leave ruts that mislead others. We aren't sure whether the trail we left in the snow was followed by other motorists. Not unreasonably, someone might have thought that this was the road to a nearby town since it was freshly traveled. I've known fathers whose anger, abuse, or negligence has caused their children to follow the wrong path. The father might get back on track, but the children might not. King David's sin of adultery affected four of his sons, each destroyed by the impact of their father's sin. The trail we leave is incredibly important for others.

Finally, we also learned that there is no convenient time to change directions. We debated where we should turn around, whether it was even feasible. Even after we knew we were on the wrong road, we continued, hoping that at some point we would come to a sign of civilization. Again, many people are so entangled in a web of deceit, lies, and broken promises that turning around seems impossible. The devil wants us to invest so much time and energy into his agenda that we feel it is too late to reverse our trajectory. So we think it is better to plunge headlong into destruction than try to make a U-turn on the road of life. Only when the desire to change is more pressing than maintaining the status quo will we change directions.

The good news: As long as you are alive, there is the possibility of "turning around," that is, of turning to a God who changes the human heart. Yes, it is better late than never, better that you enter the path of life now, no matter how many years you have been on the path of destruction. Thankfully, God often intercepts those who are traveling on the wrong road. He gives them strength to change and rewards them with undeserved grace.

MAKING A BAD MAN GOOD

Immanuel Kant, a philosopher of the German Enlightenment, asked, "How can a man who is by nature bad, become good?" As I write, the news has just been reported that all of the so-called Texas Seven jail escapees have been captured (one committed suicide). Could even these hardened criminals, accused of capital crimes, be made good? More jail time certainly will not do it. Sheer determination will not do it. Rehabilitation is out of the question. But what man can't do, God can.

The Bible teaches that though we can change our behavior, we cannot change our hearts; we cannot give ourselves desires that conform to God's ways. "Can the Ethiopian change his skin or the leopard its spots? Neither can you do good who are accustomed to doing evil" (Jer. 13:23). There are some things we can do; there are some things only God can do. And blessed is he who knows the difference! But not everyone will take advantage of God's power—many will die with the stain of guilt upon their conscience.

Yes, there is hope for those who want it, but we cannot force people to accept what they do not desire. On more than one occasion parents have brought a wayward teenager to my office and said, in effect, "Here he is; fix him." But I cannot "fix" someone who does not want to be fixed. Even God Himself often backs away from those who are determined to take their own path. Several hundred years before Christ, one of the tribes of Israel had become so corrupt that God said, "Ephraim is joined to idols; leave him alone!" (Hos. 4:17).

So if you ask me, "Is there hope for a particular philanderer, control freak,or criminal? Will the rapist be given a repentant heart? Will the thief seek restitution and the stalker surrender to the police? Will the child reared in a Christian home leave the drug culture and return to the God of his parents?" the honest but painful answer is "I don't know." There are no guarantees.

What we do know is that though some changes can arise from within us, transformation cannot. We must have something implanted within us that we were not born with; it has to be a miracle of God. Imagine a leopard hating his spots because he wants to resemble a lion; but alas, he cannot change his skin, and neither can we change our hearts.

Yes, of course people sometimes change their behavior on their own, especially with the help of counseling, support groups, and will power. But what they cannot do is take the spots (stain) of their sin away; nor can they change their fundamental desires. Though they might drop a destructive habit, their view of the world and God is unchanged. They might admire holiness, but they do not love it; they might worship God, but they do not love Him. God alone can give us the ability to hate our sin and desire Himself above all else.

That said, anyone can be changed by God, if they so desire. We read, "I will sprinkle clean water on you, and you will be clean; I will cleanse you from all your impurities and from all your idols. I will give you a new heart and put a new spirit in you; I will remove from you your heart of stone and give you a heart of flesh. And I will put my Spirit in you and move you to follow my decrees and be careful to keep my laws" (Ezek. 36:25–27). This is a magnificent promise.

God can cleanse our hearts!

God can re-create our hearts!

God can put His Spirit into our hearts!

The transformation of the desires is one of the surest signs that we have experienced what Jesus calls the "new birth," without which we cannot see the kingdom of heaven. God's work in the human heart is not superficial; it reaches to the core of our being and changes us from the inside out. At our conversion, by an act of creation, something exists within us that was not there before. As I mentioned, our love for sin is replaced by a love for God; our desire to fulfill the passions of the flesh has been replaced with a desire to be filled with God's Spirit. Formerly, we disdained the Bible as a crude book of laws; now we "delight in the law of the Lord" and want to meditate on it day and night.

At last we have an answer to Kant's question: Can a man who by nature is bad be made good? The answer is yes, if God implants a new heart within him. "Therefore, if anyone is in Christ, he is a new creation; the old has gone, the new has come!" (2 Cor. 5:17).

Some people find all of their base desires instantly changed when they are converted by God through faith in Christ. I know people who have emptied their bottles of alcohol into the sink, never to desire alcohol again. Others find that habits such as using pornography, gambling, and sexual addiction drop by the wayside as dead leaves from a tree. Understandably so, for "the old has gone, the new has come." They know what Paul meant when he wrote, "I have been crucified with Christ and I no longer live, but Christ lives in me. The life I live in the body, I live by faith in the Son of God, who loved me and gave himself for me" (Gal. 2:20).

Others find, however, that their struggle with sin only intensifies after their conversion. Whereas before they did as they pleased without thought of whether God approved, now they desire to please Him and are grieved when they fall back into their former behavioral ruts. What is more, Satan, who was quite content while they were in his column, now mounts an arsenal of opposition in the form of inflamed temptations, doubts, and despair.

To put it differently: Before our conversion, Mr. Hyde rules our lives with only respectful deference to Dr. Jekyll; after our conversion, Mr. Hyde is to submit to the control of the Holy Spirit, who indwells all those who have come to faith in Christ. Conflict is inevitable. Indeed, the apostle Paul himself described the struggle within his own heart: "We know that the law is spiritual; but I am unspiritual, sold as a slave to sin. I do not understand what I do. For what I want to do I do not do, but what I hate I do" (Rom. 7:14–15). We've all done what we did not want to do because we did not have the power to do what we wanted to do!

Yes, Christians—good Christians, if you please—can do some very bad things.

Once a person is born again, he begins the fight for holiness, a commitment to purity, and a new love for God. But success is not automatic;

he must begin the disciplines of the Christian life: Bible reading, prayer, and the fellowship of the church. For the new desires must constantly struggle against the old desires associated with the past life.

If you ask the ultimate question, Why will some people have a radical change after their conversion while others fall back into former habits? I cannot answer. I've often puzzled as to why two people reared in the same home with the same advantages travel down separate paths, one righteous and the other evil. The reasons for the difference of disposition are known, but only to God. All that we can say is that it is never a matter of God's inability; it is always a matter of man's unwillingness.

TRUE CONVERSION

To illustrate the radical nature of conversion, let us think back to the life of a man named Paul, the author of many of the books of the New Testament. He became, by all accounts, a man of great integrity, a man of prayer and faith, a man who was mightily used by God to plant churches and encourage believers, a man to whom the great doctrines of our faith were revealed.

But it wasn't always that way. Listen to his own testimony:

> I thank Christ Jesus our Lord, who has given me strength, that he considered me faithful, appointing me to his service. Even though I was once a blasphemer and a persecutor and a violent man, I was shown mercy because I acted in ignorance and unbelief. The grace of our Lord was poured out on me abundantly, along with the faith and love that are in Christ Jesus. (1 Tim. 1:12–14)

I was a *blasphemer!* I was a *persecutor!* I was *violent!* He was a blasphemer because he adamantly spoke against Jesus and denied that He was the Messiah. Before his conversion the notion of a crucified Savior was a contradiction in terms. The Book of Deuteronomy declares that a man who is hanged is cursed (see Deut. 21:23). The Messiah was One who was favored with divine blessing, not with a divine curse. So Paul saw Christianity as a malignant growth that necessitated radical surgery.

Second, Paul was a persecutor. His first encounter with the growing Christian movement was as a zealot who intended to stamp out the faith. Later he would say, "I am the least of the apostles . . . because I persecuted the church of God" (1 Cor. 15:9; see also Gal. 1:13). We read that when he left Jerusalem for Damascus to arrest Christians he was "breathing out murderous threats against the Lord's disciples" (Acts 9:1). He was a ravenous enemy of the faith, arresting and imprisoning men and women and endeavoring to make them renounce their faith in the presence of the synagogue courts.[2] His passion was to crush the faith in the bud.

Third, he was "a man of insolent and brutal violence," as the Greek text puts it. The word is *hubristes*, a kind of arrogant sadism. Aristotle gives this definition: "Hubris means to hurt and to grieve people in such a way that shame comes to the man who is hurt or grieved . . . and this is done simply because the man finds delight in his own cruelty and in the suffering of the other person."[3] In short, Paul took a sadistic delight in inflicting pain. He was not content with words of insult; he was not content with legal persecution but went to the limits of calculated brutality. That is why he spoke of himself not merely as the one who was the chief of sinners, but as the one who still *is* the chief of sinners. The memory of his sin kept him humble.

En route to Damascus with a letter in his hand giving him permission to extradite fugitives, he was intercepted by the risen Christ! The details are as follows: "As he neared Damascus on the journey, suddenly a light from heaven flashed around him. He fell to the ground and heard a voice say to him, 'Saul, Saul, why do you persecute me?'" (Acts 9:3). This was not just an experience within his mind. He both saw Christ and spoke with Him; it was a revelation directly from heaven to a man walking with his associates along a trail. His experience was so real that he put it on a par with the resurrection appearances that the disciples experienced. When his apostolic credentials were questioned, he asked, "Have I not seen Jesus our Lord?" (1 Cor. 9:1).

With no conscious preparation, Paul found himself instantaneously compelled by what he saw and heard to acknowledge that Jesus of Nazareth, the crucified One, was the promised Messiah, alive after His passion, vindicated and exalted by God. And, much to his surprise, this was the Lord who was conscripting him into His service.[4] There could be no resisting of the divine will and purpose.

He was blinded by excessive light, so he was led into Damascus to the house of one Judas in the street called Straight, where arrangements had been made for him to lodge. There he was visited by Ananias, one of the local disciples, who greeted him as a fellow brother and disciple of Jesus. No conversion was as dramatic; no conversion so quickly turned a man from the hater of the Christian religion to a lover of it. Back in the eighteenth century G. Lyttelton wrote, "The conversion and apostleship of St. Paul alone, duly considered, was of itself a demonstration sufficient to prove Christianity to be a divine religion."[5]

Two things happened. First, he had to change his mind about who Jesus was; that is the first step in conversion. He realized that Jesus is the Son of God; God of very God. He was convinced that it is not contradictory to believe that Jesus was both the promised Messiah and the One who was cursed on the cross.

But second, he also had his nature changed; the transformation was not intellectual only, but also included a changed heart. Something happened in his mind, but something also happened to his desires. Conversion brings about a change in both the head and the heart.

New Affections

During the 1700s, when a revival spread in New England, critics insisted that it was nothing more than a man-made religious phenomenon based on emotions and mass hysteria. To defend the revival and to raise the level of discernment among the people, theologian Jonathan Edwards wrote a book titled *Religious Affections*, which addressed the question of how we can know one's conversion was genuine. He agreed with the critics in this sense, that Satan imitates spiritual experiences, making people think they are converted because they prayed a prayer or had an emotional moment of exuberance. Edwards feared, as I do, that members of his own congregation who thought they were saved would discover in the day of judgment that they were eternally lost.

But Edwards also believed that many conversions are genuine. They cannot be explained as the result of religious fervor or the excitement of overzealous well-wishers. The question before him was: What are the marks of true conversion? In his book he argues that the chief sign of true conversion is a change in our affections, that is, a change in our desires. When we are converted, God implants a new love within us. Obviously, no one can make himself love God or for that matter, love his enemy. We cannot wake up in the morning and say, "Beginning today I will love the Lord my God with all my heart, mind, and soul." We can change our habits, but not our hearts.

These new affections can arise only because God implants them in us at conversion. And though we continue to struggle with sin and failure, though we experience depression and doubt, there is within all believers a fundamental reorientation of affections. Love cannot be turned on and off like a faucet; just ask the heartbroken lover who intended to marry his beloved but she said no. He wishes he had a love switch, but he cannot will the feelings away. His heart will override all rational considerations and go on loving, no matter what. Love dies a slow and painful death. It is one thing to change what a man believes, but it is quite another to change what he loves.

If a bad man is to be made good, he must turn from his love of evil to a new love for God. True conversion reaches down to what Edwards called the "affections." Affections must be distinguished from emotions. Emotions fluctuate, whereas what we hate and what we love are, for the most part, constant. All true believers have a God-implanted love for Christ. "Though you have not seen him, you love him; and even though you do not see him now, you believe in him and are filled with an inexpressible and glorious joy" (1 Pet. 1:8). Only God can cause us to love someone we have not seen!

Obviously, many conversions fall short of the real thing. There are false conversions accompanied by zeal and a change of habits, but these changes might be brought about by influences other than the Holy Spirit. What is missing is a fervent love for Christ and "an abiding sense of sin."[6] For the true Christian lives a life of continual submission and repentance. And, says Edwards, "for man must first love God and be one with Him in heart before he will esteem God's good as his own."[7]

The bottom line: The love and pursuit of holiness is the mark of the true Christian. According to Edwards, Christians are convinced of the beauty of the God who has revealed Himself to them; thus, they delight in Him and want to be like Him. Personal holiness is the purpose and goal of salvation. "But just as he who called you is holy, so be holy in all you do; for it is written: 'Be holy, because I am holy'" (1 Pet. 1:15). God alone is able to overcome our natural aversion to holiness and give us a love for that which we once despised.

In contrast, the unconverted do not love God. They want to use Him; they want to benefit from Him. If they think He answers prayer, they are interested, for they are anxious to further their own desires and agenda. But they do not see God's loveliness; they do not love Him for Himself. In fact, they will redefine Him to suit their own interests and desires. But conversion causes us to love God and His holiness. It follows that there can be no assurance of salvation based on a past experience alone. We must expect a continuing work of God in the heart that confirms one's faith.

By nature the unconverted have no hunger for the Scriptures. They might study the Bible—indeed, there are some scholars, such as those of the Jesus Seminar, who spend their lives dissecting the text. But they see the Bible as an interesting historical book, not as a place to which they come to feed their souls. They cannot say, "Oh, how I love your law! I meditate on it all day long. Your commands make me wiser than my enemies" (Ps. 119:97–98).

The happiness of the unconverted is found in circumstances, not in

God. They seek new experiences, new ways of self-enhancement, since self-love is the motivation of the human heart. They might turn to God for help when their lives fall apart, but when all is going well, they would never think of finding their joy in Him. They simply cannot relate to commands such as, "Delight yourself in the LORD and he will give you the desires of your heart" (Ps. 37:4).

Of course Edwards lists many other tests, but the central point is that we love according to our nature; we love that which fulfills our desires. Before our conversion we had nothing in common with God, but thanks to Jesus, who had something in common with us, we have been reconciled to God. Now "our fellowship is with the Father and with his Son, Jesus Christ" (1 John 1:3). We love Him because through conversion we are "partakers of the divine nature" and His life has been wrought within us. Thus our love is God-directed.

To return to Paul: Christ not only saved him, but also trusted him with the ministry of the gospel. The persecutor of the church now became an ambassador of the church. There is a story about a Spartan wrestler at the Olympic games who was offered a large bribe if he would let his opponent win. But he refused the offer and won after a personally costly victory. He fought, he said, so he would have "the privilege of standing in front of my king in battle." His reward was to serve and, if need be, to die for his king. Conversion means that we have such a love, not for an earthly king, but for the King of kings.

WHAT GOD CAN DO

So what *can* God do? He changed the beliefs and desires of Paul, who went from trying to exterminate the Christian sect to promoting it. Paul went from being a passionate lover of religion to being a passionate lover of God. Christ personally came out of heaven to convert him; possibly no one else would ever have shared the good news with him. God chose him not because he was a good man, but because He wanted to use him as an example of "a bad man made good."

Paul wrote, "I was shown mercy because I acted in ignorance and unbelief. The grace of our Lord was poured out on me abundantly, along with the faith and love that are in Christ Jesus" (1 Tim. 1:13–14). When he says he was "shown mercy," he uses the passive form of the verb; that is, he received mercy because he persecuted the church ignorantly. The Old Testament did make a distinction between willful sins and those done in ignorance, but even those done in ignorance had to be forgiven.

Paul continues, "The grace of our Lord was poured out on me abundantly." In Greek the word *grace* has the prefix *huper-* (the word comes to us today as *hyper;* we know that a child who is superactive is *hyper*active, so a person who needs much grace needs *hyper*grace). So Paul says there is *super*grace for *super*sinners. Everyone needs grace; some need superabounding grace.

If mercy is withholding the judgment we deserve, grace is receiving a gift we do not deserve. John Newton, who penned the words to "Amazing Grace," wrote his own epitaph, which read, "John Newton, Clerk, once an Infidel and a Libertine, a Servant of Slaves in Africa, was by the Mercy of our Lord and Savior Jesus Christ, Preserved, Restored, Pardoned and Appointed to Preach the Faith he had so long labored to destroy." (There is nothing wrong with remembering our sins, just as long as we are not questioning whether we have been forgiven of them.)

What is the requirement for us to experience this grace, the grace that converts us and gives us a "new heart"? We must transfer our trust to Christ alone, for "to all who received him, to those who believed in his name, he gave the right to become children of God—children born not of natural descent, nor of human decision or a husband's will, but born of God" (John 1:12–13). Augustine was right when he said we would never seek for God unless He had already found us first.

When we exercise faith, God credits the righteousness of Christ to our account and we are declared to be as righteous as Christ Himself; thus we are reconciled to God. The issue, therefore, is not the greatness of our sin, but the quality of the righteousness that we receive from

God. God does not find it more difficult to forgive "bigger" sinners than "lesser" ones. In either case God must supply the righteousness and create within them a new heart.

We think that Paul's conversion was unusual, since we have not seen the risen Christ. We were not called to be apostles, to reveal new doctrines of the faith. But Paul said that what happened to him was an "outline sketch" of the miracle that God would perform in the lives of all who believed. He writes, "But for that very reason I was shown mercy so that in me, the worst of sinners, Christ Jesus might display his unlimited patience as an example for those who would believe on him and receive eternal life" (1 Tim. 1:16). The word for "example" is *hupotuposis*, which means a first draft, a preliminary model, a pattern. Paul is saying, "Look what happened to me! If I can be rescued, forgiven, and have my affections changed, there is hope for anyone!"

Paul sees himself as one whose sins called forth the most gracious mercy of God. But we are saved by the same gracious mercy. The better we know God, the greater our sins become and the greater God's grace appears.

If you, dear reader, have never been converted, call out to God at this moment and ask Him to save you. Specifically, if you believe that when Jesus died on the cross He did all that ever will be necessary for you to stand in God's holy presence—if you accept Christ as your personal sin-bearer—you will be saved.

GOOD NEWS FOR GREAT SINNERS

Despite three decades of studying guilt, responsibility, and the nature of evil, Gritta Sereny was not prepared for the uproar that ensued when she published her book, *Cries Unheard*. The book is the story of Mary Bell, who at the age of eleven murdered two little boys and then appeared, in the eyes of Britain, to have no remorse.

Ms. Sereny said of her critics, "Behind their reaction is the idea of the Devil, the idea of evil. . . . This is the belief that the evil person is evil, period. There's no rehabilitation, no redemption. This is a Christian nation, but the Christianity stops short of redemption."[8]

Ms. Sereny is both right and wrong. She is wrong to suggest that evil did not reside in the heart of the little girl who killed the two boys, but she is right in saying that a Christianity that stops short of redemption is not a Christianity at all. Yes, even those who don't seem to have remorse can be changed, for there is a redemption that goes to the heart of the calloused heart. No one has fallen so far but that God can reach him.

We play no part in our conversion; indeed, God even grants us the ability to receive His free gift. But we do play a part in our triumph over sin. Salvation must be received, but personal victory, with God's help, must be won. For that, we need to learn to fight against all the forces that are arrayed against us. The church, the body of Christ, must help us in growing in our love for God and in our walk in His Word.

Can God make an evil man "good"? Back in 1977, New York was terrorized by the "Son of Sam," a murderer who stalked and killed women. Time and again he would strike, leaving not a trace and leaving the police dumbfounded. After thirteen months, David Berkowitz, a twenty-four-year-old postal worker, was arrested. In court he pled guilty to killing five women and one man and wounding many others.

Pastor Jim Cymbala, who was in New York at the time, had forgotten about him until he received a call from a woman saying that Berkowitz had become a Christian and requested a visit. They talked on the phone several times and exchanged letters. His story was sad indeed: He had become involved in Satanism, violence, and evil of every kind. To quote his words, "Nothing could control me. I was like the tormented Gadarene demoniac—anguished, inflicting pain on myself, and driven to dark and lonely places."[9] Thanks to the witness of a fellow prisoner, Berkowitz knelt by his bunk and accepted Christ as Savior. He is progressing in his faith and is a diligent student of God's Word. He is now an assistant to the chaplain. He has become a dear friend to the Cymbalas and continues to witness in prison. He has never asked for parole, because he knows that the crimes he committed are so bad that he deserves to spend the rest of his life in prison.

I'm reminded of the words of Corrie ten Boom: "There is no pit so deep, but that God is deeper still." "Call to me and I will answer you and tell you great and unsearchable things you do not know" (Jer. 33:3). Thankfully, even today, God still makes bad men good.

A Promise to Ponder

Yet to all who received him, to those who believed in his name,
he gave the right to become children of God—Children born not of
natural descent, nor of human decision or a husband's will,
but born of God.

—JOHN 1:12–13

ENDNOTES

Introduction

1. *Time,* 18 October 1999, 47.
2. James M. Houston, ed., *The Mind on Fire: An Anthology of the Writings of Blaise Pascal* (Portland, Oreg.: Multnomah, 1989), 113.
3. "The Philosophical Brothel," *Rutherford,* January 1997, vol. 6, no. 1, 18.
4. Jeremy Miller, "Is There a Gene for the Soul?" *Chicago Tribune,* 2 July 2000, Perspective, 1.

Chapter 1

1. Lynn Vincent, "Here We Go Again," *World,* 11 November 2000, 18.
2. Mark Epstein, "Living Behind the Mask," *Oprah* magazine, vol. 1, no. 5, November 2000, 215.
3. M. Scott Peck, *People of the Lie* (New York: Touchtone Books, 1983), 60. Although this book is not based on a biblical understanding of man, it provides provocative insights on the nature of evil. Though excellent in analysis, it lacks a compelling rationalization of the need for forgiveness and reconciliation with God.
4. Dorie Vanstone and Erwin Lutzer, *Dorie: The Girl Nobody Loved* (Chicago: Moody Press, 1979), 15.

5. Adam Smith, quoted in *Self-Deception and Self-Understanding—New Essays in Philosophy and Psychology,* Mike Martin, ed. (University of Kansas Press, 1985), 138.

Chapter 2

1. Robert S. McGee, *The Search for Significance,* James Houston, ed. (Portland, Oreg.: Multnomah, 1989), 115.
2. Ibid., 23.
3. James Houston, ed., *The Mind on Fire, An Anthology of the Writings of Blaise Pascal* (Portland, Oreg.: Multnomah, 1989), 115.
4. Geoffrey Kelly and Burton Nelson, eds., *A Testament to Freedom, The Essential Writings of Dietrich Bonhoeffer* (San Francisco: Harper, 1994), 218.

Chapter 3

1. George Stephanopolous, *All Too Human—A Political Education* (New York; London: Little, Brown & Co., 1999), 4.
2. Quoted in *Modern Reformation,* January/February 2001, 13.
3. Henry J. Rogers, *The Silent War* (Nashville: Thomas Nelson, 2000), 156.
4. Louis McBurney, "Avoiding the Scarlet Letter," *Leadership,* Summer 1985, 46.

Chapter 4

1. Richard Dortch, *Integrity: How I Lost It, and My Journey Back* (Green Forest, Ark.: New Leaf Press, 1992).
2. *Time,* 20 December 1999, 46.
3. James Peterson and Peter Kim, *The Day America Told the Truth* (New York: Plume, 1992), 7.
4. Ibid., 45.
5. Ibid., 65–66.

6. Ibid., 38.
7. Ibid., 62.
8. Ibid., 34.
9. Ibid., 73.
10. William Shakespeare, *Macbeth* (2.2.60–67).
11. Richard Dortch, *Secrets of the Heart* (Green Forest, Ark.: New Leaf Press, 1996), 110.

Chapter 5

1. Thomas Merton, *Thoughts in Solitude* (New York: Farrar, Straus, Giroux, 1956), 92.
2. Quoted in Martin, *Self-Deception and Self-Understanding*, 30.
3. Arthur Guiterman, quoted in *Leadership*, Summer 1986, 40.
4. Lewis Smeeds, *Shame and Grace: Healing the Hurts We Don't Deserve* (San Francisco: HarperSanFrancisco/Zondervan, 1993), quoted in *Christianity Today*, 15 October, 1993, 72.
5. John Bradshaw, *Healing the Shame That Binds You* (Deerfield Beach, Fla.: Health Communications, 1993), 23. My description of the characteristics and effects of a shame-based home is largely derived from this book. Helpful though it is, the book fails to adequately address objective shame and the need for forgiveness and cleansing from God.
6. Ibid., 40.
7. Ibid., 44.
8. Ibid., 47.
9. Ibid., 19.
10. Ibid., 88.
11. Ibid.
12. Ibid., 97.
13. Smeeds, *Shame and Grace*, 72.
14. Rodney Clapp, "Shame Crucified," *Christianity Today*, 11 March 1991, 28.

15. Ibid., paraphrase.
16. Ibid., 28.
17. Ted Roberts, *Pure Desire* (Ventura, Calif.: Regal, 1999), 42.

Chapter 6

1. Quoted in Joan Winfrey, "Tantrums! And Tyrants: Understanding Children's Anger," *Focal Point,* a publication of Denver Seminary.
2. *Time,* 9 August 1999, 26.
3. Paul Hegstrom, *Angry Men and the Women Who Love Them* (Kansas City: Beacon Hill, 1999), 26.
4. Ibid.
5. Ibid., 9–10.
6. Ibid.
7. Mark Cosgrove, *Counseling for Anger* (Dallas: Word, 1988), 23.

Chapter 7

1. The story of Hemingway is summarized from Daniel Pawley, "Ernest Hemingway: Tragedy of an Evangelical Family," *Christianity Today,* 23 November 1984, 20–27.
2. Ibid., 23.
3. Ibid., 24.
4. United States Bureau of Census, Current Population Reports, Household and Family Characteristics: March 1988, 515.
5. Barbara Walters, interview with Patrick Jephson, *20/20,* 6 October 2000.
6. Ibid.
7. Kansas City: National Center for Fathering, 1999.
8. Brennan Manning, *Abba's Child* (Colorado Springs: NavPress, 1994), 15, 16.
9. Ibid., 131.

10. David Stoop, *Making Peace with Your Father* (Wheaton, Ill.: Tyndale, 1992), 223.
11. Ibid., 234.
12. Manning, *Abba's Child,* 121.

Chapter 8

1. Martin, *Self-Deception and Self-Understanding,* 11.
2. Patrick Carnes, *Out of the Shadows—Understanding Sexual Addiction* (Minneapolis: CompCare Publishers, 1983), 64.
3. Craig Nakken, *The Addictive Personality* (Center City, Minn.: Hazelden, 1998), 1.
4. Carnes, *Out of the Shadows,* 7.
5. Ibid., v.

Chapter 9

1. Les Carter, *Heartfelt Change* (Chicago: Moody Press, 1993), 160.
2. Melody Beattie, *Codependent No More* (Center City, Minn.: Hazelden, 1992), 81.
3. Peck, *People of the Lie,* 75–76.
4. Ibid., 76.
5. Ibid., 47.
6. Gene Edwards, *A Tale of Three Kings* (Auburn, Maine: Christian Books, 1980), 40.
7. Ibid., 21, 22.

Chapter 10

1. Quoted in Martin, *Self-Deception and Self-Understanding,* 52.
2. Quoted in Manning, *Abba's Child,* 27.
3. Manning, *Abba's Child,* 74.

4. John Claypool as told to Ken Hyatt, "Freedom Behind Bars," *The Standard*, April 1999, 22–23.

5. Robert Fulghum, *All I Really Needed to Know I Learned in Kindergarten: Uncommon Thoughts on Common Things* (New York: Villard Books, 1988), 56–58.

Chapter 11

1. Oscar Wilde, *De Profundis*, quoted in William Barklay, *The Letters of Galatians and Ephesians* (Edinburgh: Saint Andrew's Press, 1954), 177.

2. F. F. Bruce, *Paul, Apostle of the Heart Set Free* (Grand Rapids, Mich.: Eerdmans, 1977), 69, 70.

3. Barklay, *The Letters to Timothy, Titus, and Philemon* (Edinburgh: The Saint Andrews Press, 1965), 52.

4. Bruce, *Paul, Apostle of the Heart Set Free*, 75.

5. Ibid.

6. Jonathan Edwards, *Religious Affections*, ed. James M. Houston (Minneapolis: Bethany House, 1996).

7. Ibid., 90.

8. Sarah Lyall, "Close Enough to Evil to Look Beyond It," *New York Times*, 15 August 1998, A17, A19, quoted in *Homiletics*, April 1999.

9. Jim Cymbala with Dean Merrill, *Fresh Power* (Grand Rapids, Mich.: Zondervan, 2001), 130–37.

Dr. Erwin Lutzer is senior pastor of the Moody Church in Chicago. The author of over thirty books, including the Gold Medallion award-winning *Hitler's Cross,* the CBA bestseller *One Minute After You Die,* and *Ten Lies about God,* Dr. Lutzer is a featured speaker on the Moody Broadcast Network daily radio broadcast, "Running to Win." He is also heard on the weekly broadcasts "Moody Church Hour" and "Songs in the Night." He and his wife, Rebecca, live in Chicago and are the parents of three children.

Has a lie infiltrated your beliefs about God?
If your answer is no, you'd better check again.

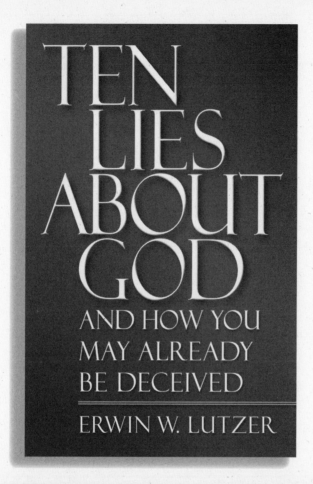

The more our post-modern society searches for God, the more it seems to draw the wrong conclusions. In *Ten Lies About God*, pastor and author Dr. Erwin Lutzer examines the reality of God as established in Scripture, dispelling the misconceptions adopted by popular culture. Accessible and insightful, Dr. Lutzer shatters false claims such as "God is more tolerant than he used to be," reveals the nature and significance of His relationship with mankind, and illuminates God's plan for the world. *Ten Lies About God* provides essential answers for a generation of seekers.

WORD PUBLISHING
NASHVILLE
www.wordpublishing.com
A Thomas Nelson Company